St. Catharines Ontario Book 5 in Colour Photos, Saving Our History One Photo at a Time

Photography
by Barbara Raué
2017

Series Name:
Cruising Ontario

Book 193: St. Catharines Book 5

Cover photo: 15 Welland Avenue, Page 36

Series Name: Cruising Ontario
Saving Our History One Photo at a Time
in colour photos

Books Available in Alphabetical Order:
Aberfoyle, Acton, Alton, Amherstburg, Ancaster, Arthur, Aylmer, Ayr, Bloomingdale, Brantford, Burlington, Caledon, Caledonia, Cambridge, Clifford, Conestogo, Delhi, Dorchester to Aylmer, Drayton, Drumbo, Dundas, Eden Mills, Elmira, Elora, Essex, Fergus, Guelph, Hagersville, Hamilton, Hanover, Harriston, Hespeler, Jarvis, Kingston, Kingsville, Kitchener, Linwood, Listowel, London, Lucknow, Mono, Mount Forest, Neustadt, New Hamburg, Niagara-on-the-Lake, Oakville, Orangeville, Orillia, Owen Sound, Palmerston, Peterborough, Petrolia, Port Elgin, Preston, Rockwood, Sarnia, Seaforth, Sheffield, Shelburne, Simcoe, Southampton, St. Jacobs, St. Marys, St. Thomas, Stoney Creek, Stratford, Thamesford, Tillsonburg, Waterdown, Waterford, Waterloo, Welland, Wellesley, Windsor, Wingham, Woodstock

Book 157: Brockville
Book 158: Merrickville
Book 159: Smiths Falls
Book 160: Portland, Newboro
Book 161: Westport & Area
Book 162: Perth
Book 163-166: Belleville
Book 167-168: Port Colborne
Book 169: Erin in Colour
Book 170: Goderich in Colour
Book 171: Sault Ste. Marie
Book 172: Lake Superior
Book 173-176: Thunder Bay
Book 177-179: Paris

Book 180: St. George
Book 182-183: Burford
Book 184: Mt Pleasant, Onondaga, Newport
Book 185-186: Grimsby
Book 187: Toronto in Colour
Book 188: Collingwood Colour
Book 189-193: St. Catharines

Other Books by Barbara Raue

Coins of Gold

Arrows, Indians and Love

The Life and Times of Barbara
Volume 1: Inventions That Have Enhanced My Life
Volume 2: Entertainment That I Have Enjoyed
Volume 3: East Coast Trips
Volume 4: Olympics Have Always Intrigued Me
Volume 5: Wonders of the World
Volume 6: Caribbean Cruises We Have Enjoyed
Volume 7: Animals
Volume 8: Storms and Other Major Disasters in My Lifetime
Volume 9: Wars, Terrorist Attacks and Major Disasters

The Cromwell Family Book

Laura Secord Discovered

Daddy Where Are You?

Montana Series
Book 1: Montana Dream
Book 2: Life on the Montana Frontier
Book 3: Montana to Boston and Back
Book 4: Montana Sons Go to War
Book 5: Montana Sons Return From War

Visit Barbara's website to view all of her books
http://barbararaue.ca

Table of Contents

Academy Street	Page 6
Lyman Street	Page 8
Court Street	Page 10
Centre Street	Page 10
Queen Street	Page 12
St. Paul Street	Page 17
Thomas Street	Page 33
Welland Avenue	Page 35
Yates Street	Page 38
Architectural Terms	Page 64
Building Styles	Page 69

St. Catharines is the largest city in Canada's Niagara Region in Southern Ontario. It is 51 kilometers (32 miles) south of Toronto across Lake Ontario, and is 19 kilometers (12 miles) inland from the international boundary with the United States along the Niagara River. It is the northern entrance of the Welland Canal.

The city was first settled by Loyalists in the 1780s. The Crown granted them land in compensation for their services and for losses in the United States. Early histories credit Sergeant Jacob Dittrick and Private John Hainer, formerly of Butler's Rangers, as among the first to come to the area. They took their Crown Patents where Dick's Creek and 12 Mile Creek merge, now the city center of St. Catharines.

Secondary to water routes, native trails provided transportation networks, resulting in the present-day radial road pattern from the City center.

The small settlement was known as "The Twelve" and as "Murray's District" to military and civic officials, but the local residents in 1796 and earlier referred to it as St. Catharines.

The Merritt family arrived; they were among the later Loyalists to relocate following the American Revolution. In 1796, Thomas Merritt arrived to build on his relationship with his former Commander and Queen's Ranger, John Graves Simcoe, now the Lieutenant Governor of Upper Canada.

The first Welland Canal was constructed from 1824 to 1833 behind what is now known as St. Paul Street, using Twelve Mile and Dick's Creek. William Hamilton Merritt worked to promote the ambitious venture, both by raising funds and by enlisting government support. The canal established St. Catharines as the hub of commerce and industry for the Niagara Peninsula.

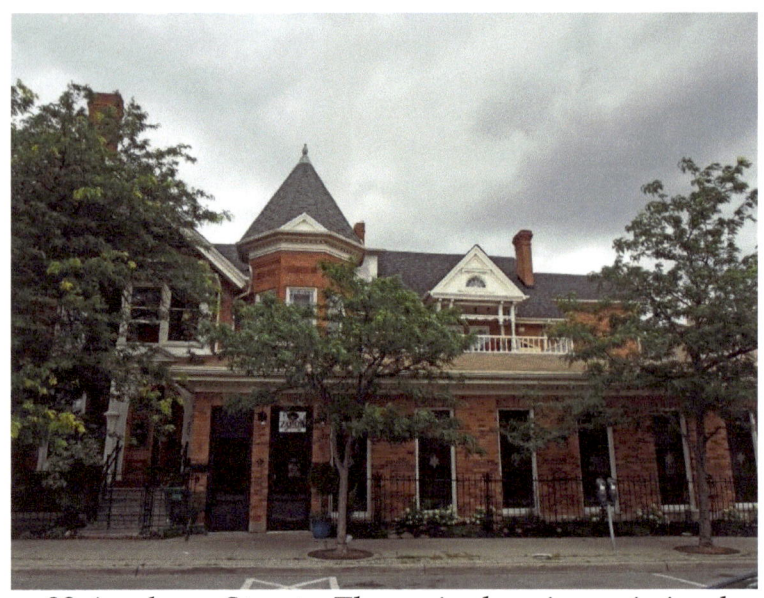

22 Academy Street – The main door is semi-circular with pilasters and a hood. It is a double three-panel door with moulded rails with a recessed panel and leaded glass with jewelled inserts. The main windows are flat and have molded trim and radiating voussoirs with large two-sash double hung windows. A turret extends from the second floor.

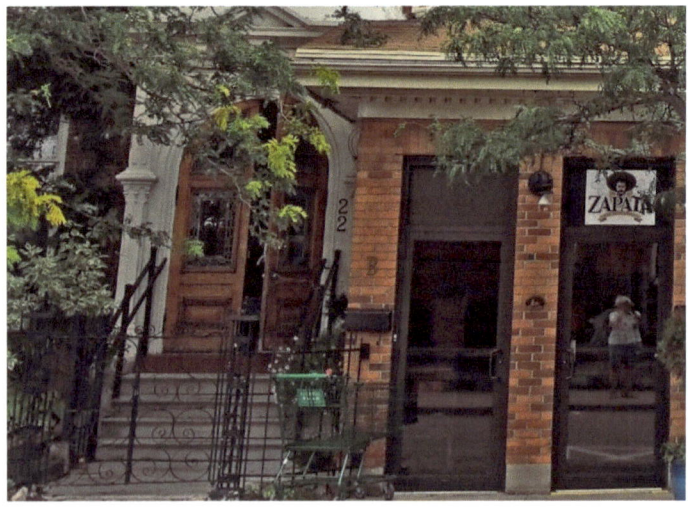

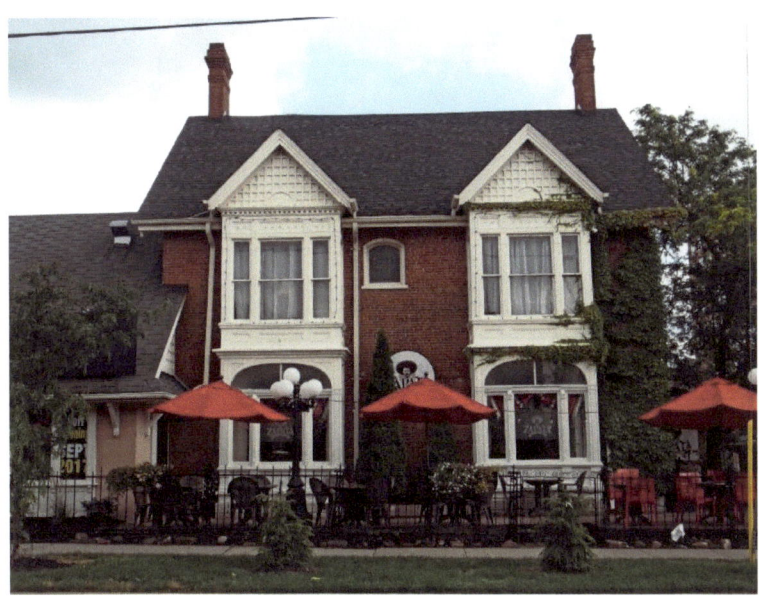

22 Academy Street – This 2½ storey Victorian style red brick building has an irregular shaped plan due to brick additions at the front, side and back. The roof is trimmed with simple bargeboards. The front dormers on the second floor have pediment roofs with one having engaged columns at the sides and a shed dormer on the uppermost level. It is now Zapata's Mexican Restaurant.

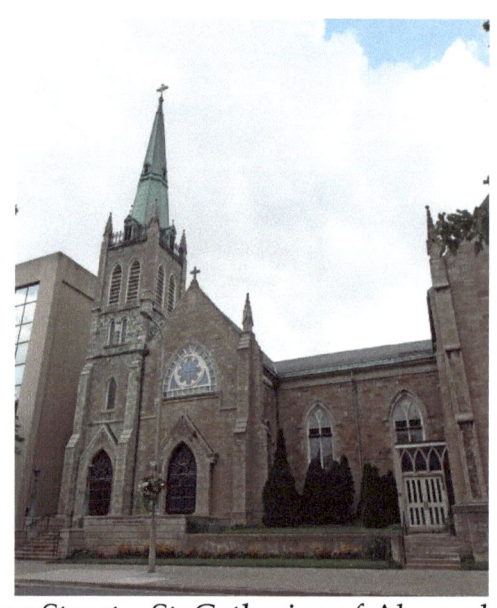

3 Lyman Street – St. Catherine of Alexandria Cathedral - The first Catholic Church at St. Catharines was built to meet the spiritual needs of the Irish labourers who built the first Welland Canal which was opened in 1829. It was a wood structure on the same site as the present Cathedral and was called St. John's because the Anglicans were already using the name St. Catherine for their church in the town of the same name.

This first Catholic Church was burned down by an arsonist on August 23, 1842. The second Welland Canal was being built between 1842 and 1845 and there were many Irish labourers in the area. Often there were delays in construction of the canal and under the guidance of their new Pastor, the Rev. Patrick McDonagh, the Irish workers used their free time to build a new parish church, this time of stone, as we can see in the structure of the present Cathedral Church. Father McDonagh laid the cornerstone on Ascension Day, May 25, 1843.

The Irish canal workers continued to build the church for the next two years. Father McDonagh opened the new church on June 10, 1845. The new church was now dedicated to St. Catherine of Alexandria - the name was now free since the Anglicans had built a new church which was dedicated to St. George, their first church also having been burnt.

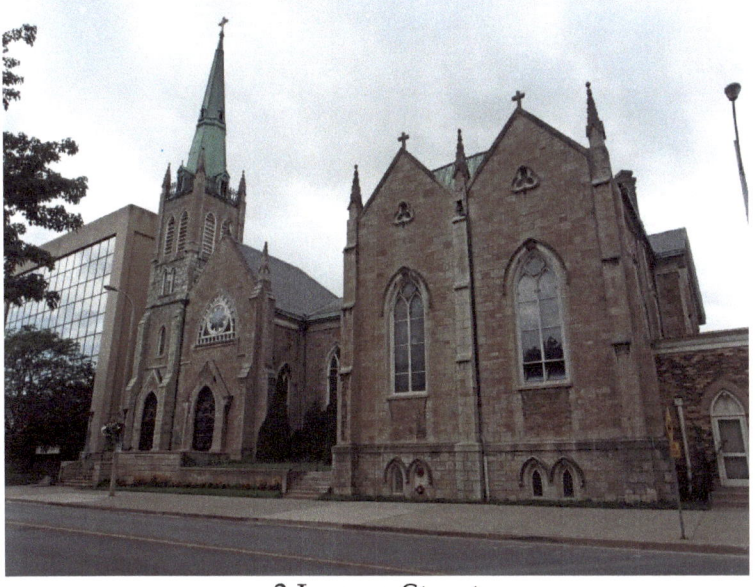

3 Lyman Street

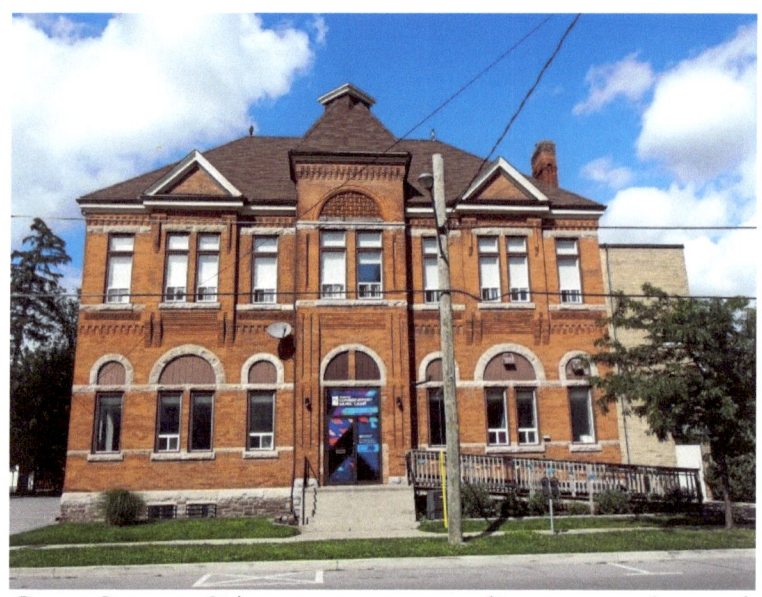

Court Street – 2½ storey tower, pediments on the roof, banding, bevelled dentil molding, semi-circular stone voussoirs,

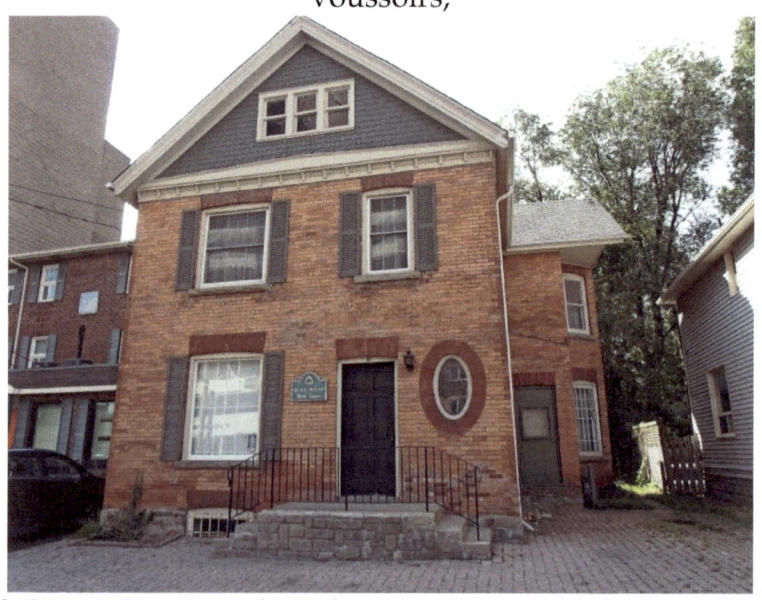

19 Centre Street – Edwardian – oval stained glass window with contrasting-colored brick voussoirs

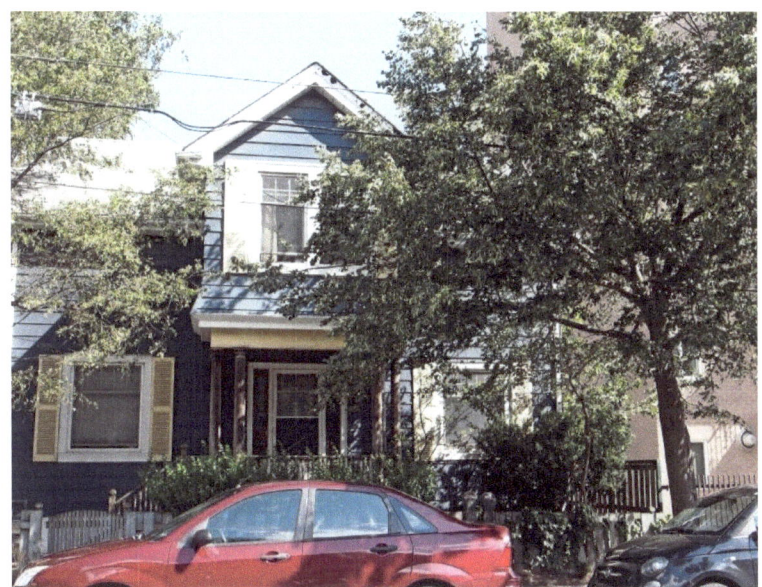

Centre Street

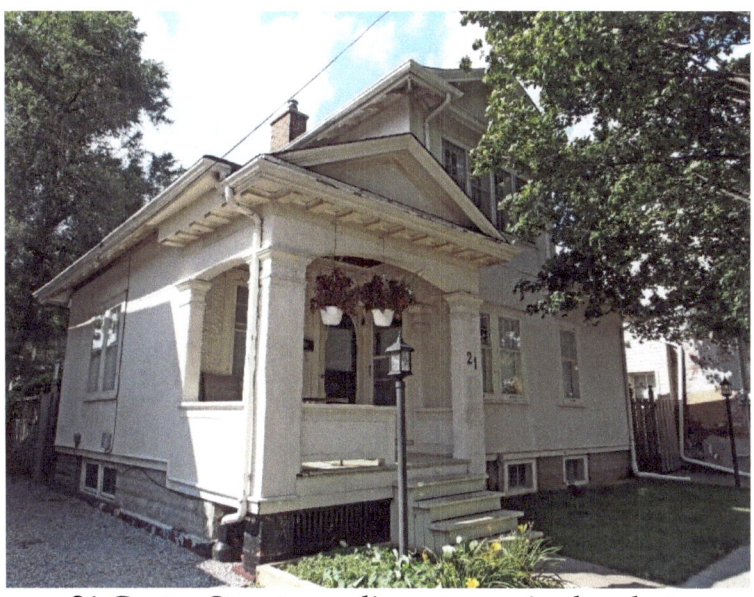

21 Centre Street – pediment, cornice brackets

Queen Street Heritage District

The Queen Street neighborhood has been subject to historical development associated with the Merritt family. The Niagara Peninsula saw considerable economic growth after the construction of the first Welland Canal, a project initiated by William Hamilton Merritt, a prominent land owner. The subdivision of his family's estate in 1868 created the Triangular Tract, a new residential neighborhood with an extensive open parcel of land known as Montebello Gardens, later to be acquired by the City as a park.

By the 1870s, Queen Street was a thriving residential street while Montebello Park saw the construction of a large pavilion and a smaller bandstand. It was not until 1913 that families settled into residential dwellings on Midland Street along the park's border. The unique building styles found in this neighborhood give the Queen Street District a diverse and rich streetscape.

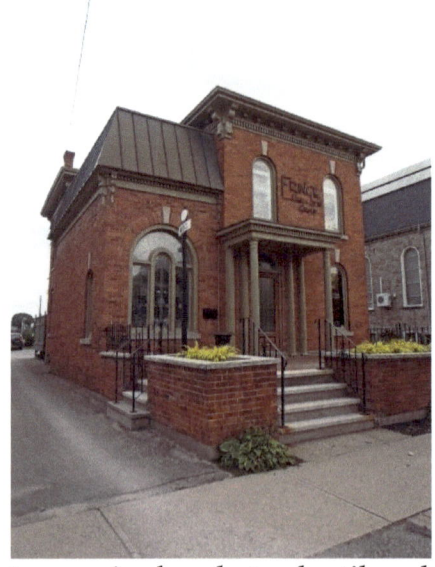

53 Queen Street – cornice brackets, dentil molding, voussoirs and keystones

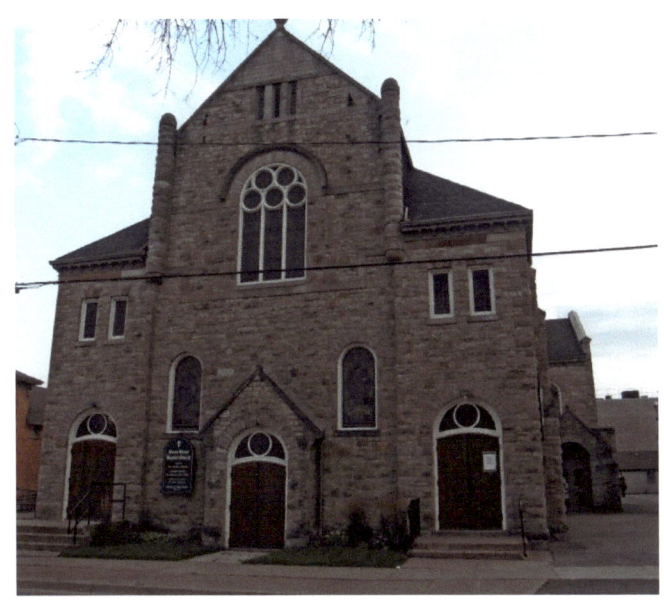

57 Queen Street – Baptist Church – 1833 – Romanesque

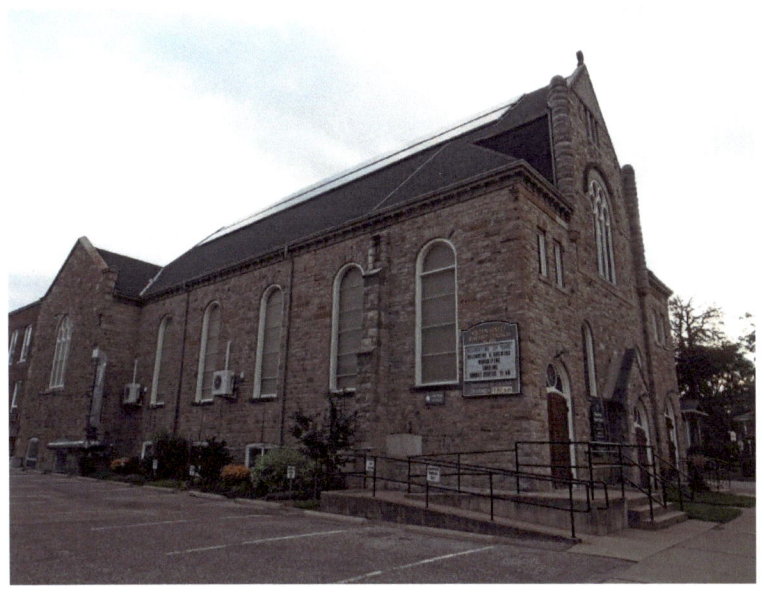

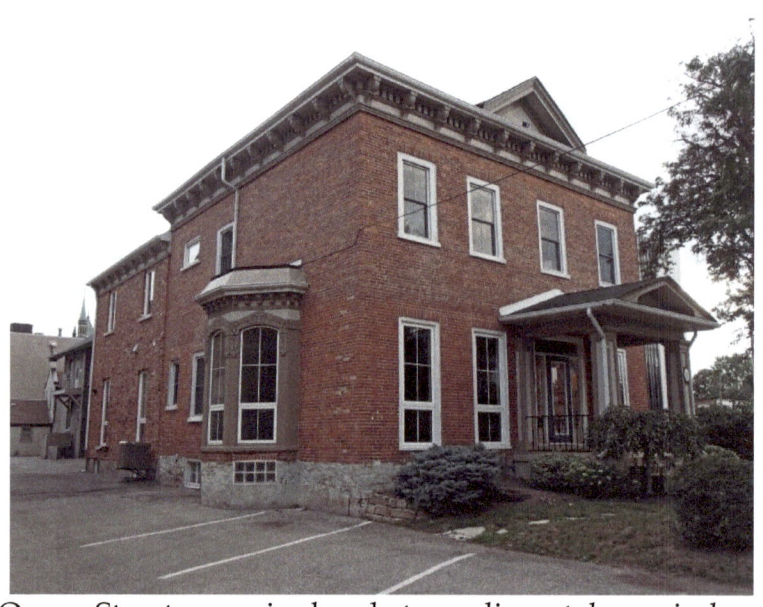

59 Queen Street – cornice brackets, pediment, bay window on side

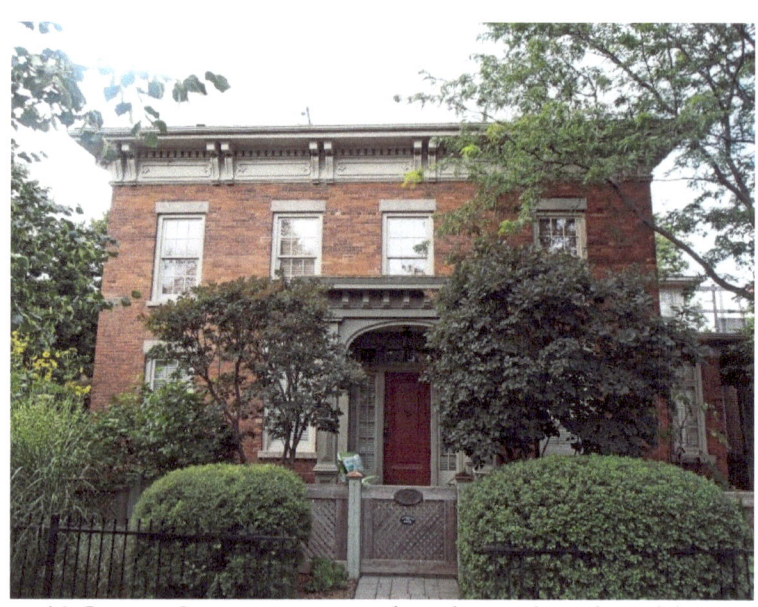

64 Queen Street – cornice brackets, dentil molding

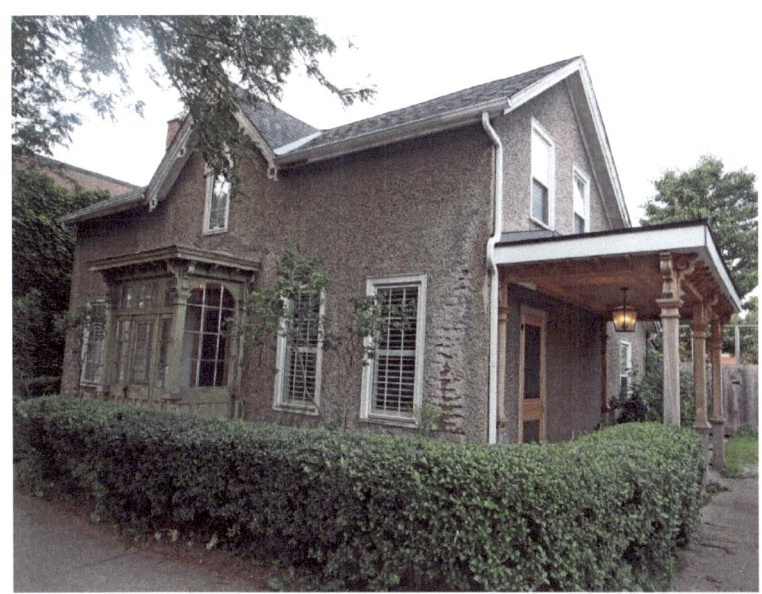

78 Queen Street – Gothic

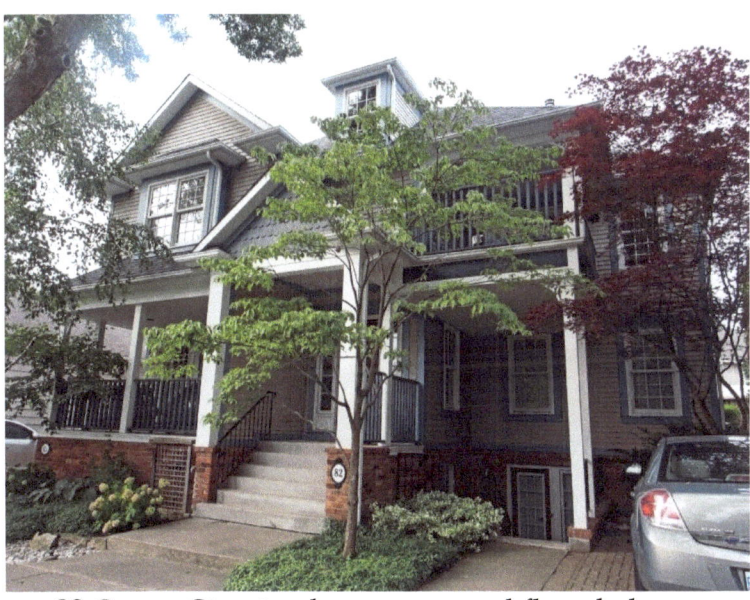

82 Queen Street – dormer, second floor balcony

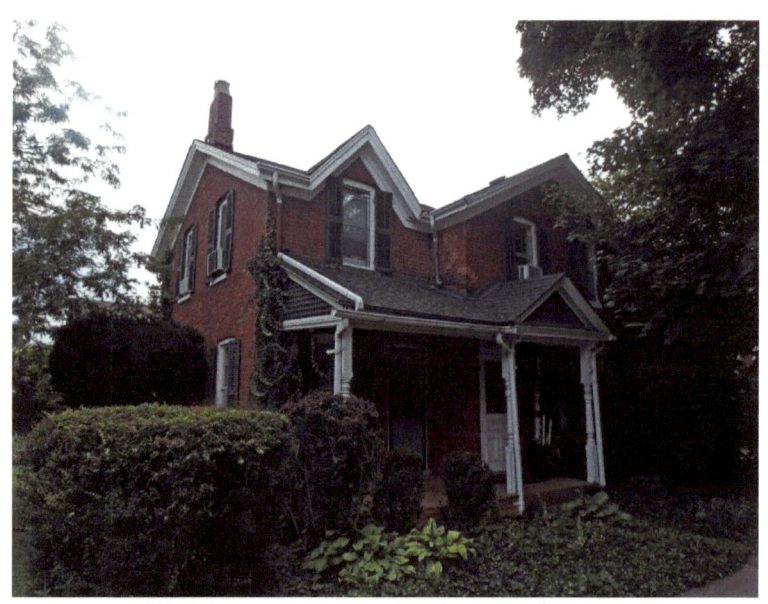

87 Queen Street – Gothic, pediment

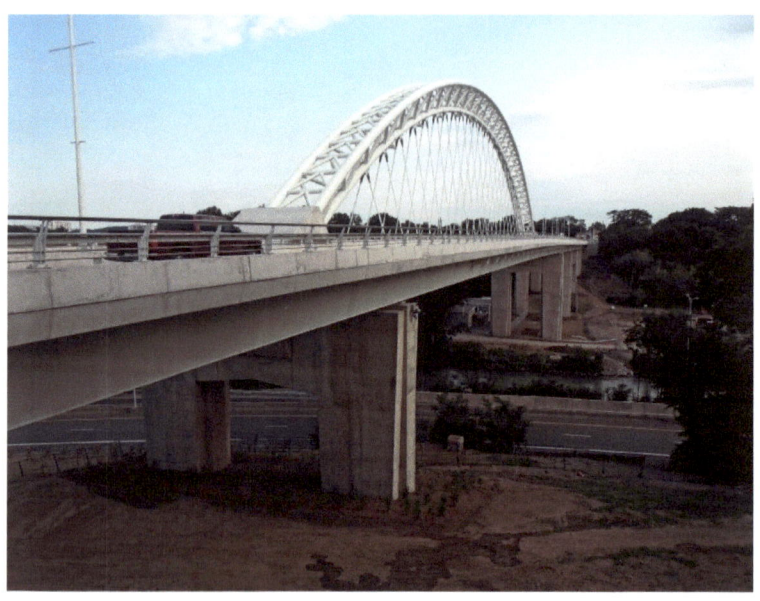

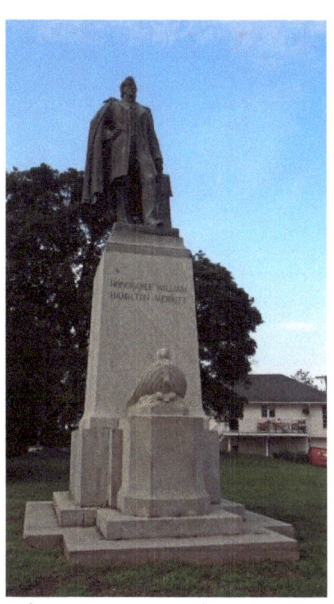

William Hamilton Merritt (1793-1862), a pioneer in the field of transportation, settled at Twelve Mile Creek (St. Catharines) with his Loyalist family in 1796. He operated mercantile and milling enterprises, and was primarily responsible for the construction of the first Welland Canal.

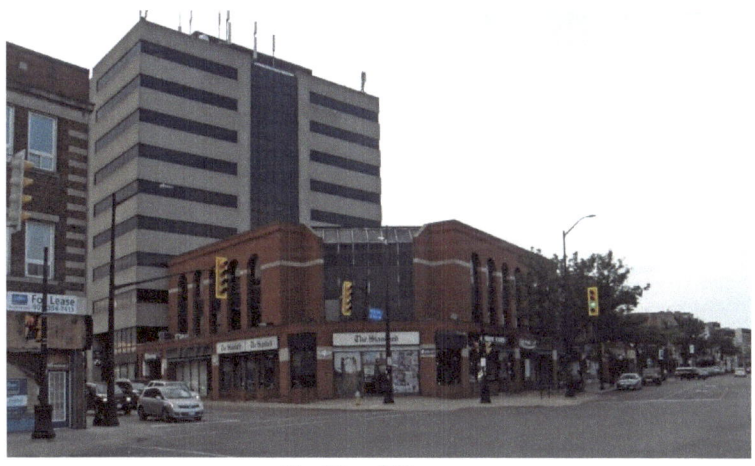

St. Paul Street

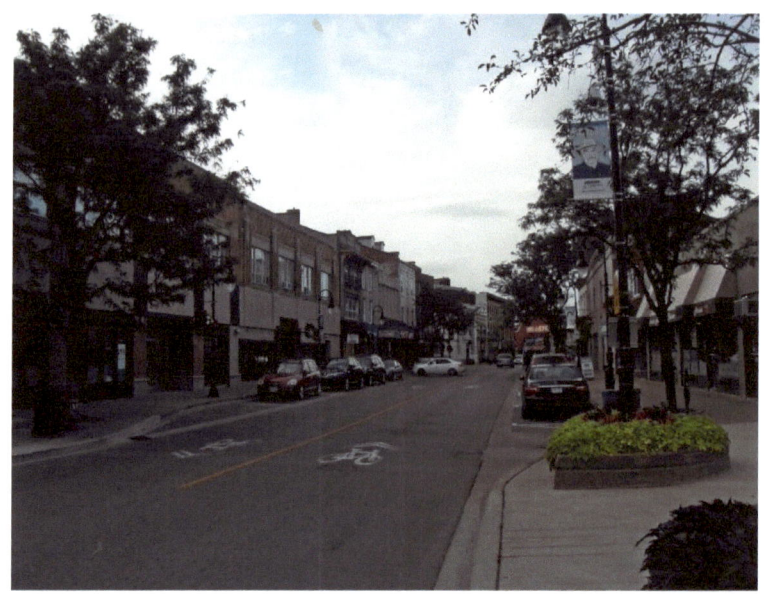

St. Paul Street

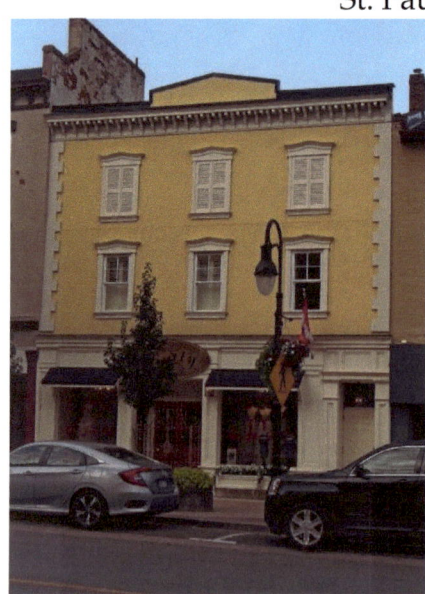 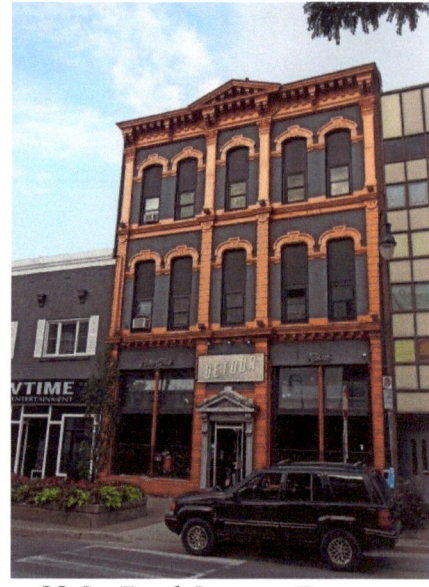

St. Paul Street
Parapet, cornice brackets,
Corner quoins

88 St. Paul Street - Detour
Music Hall – pediment,
cornice brackets, pilasters
with composite capitals

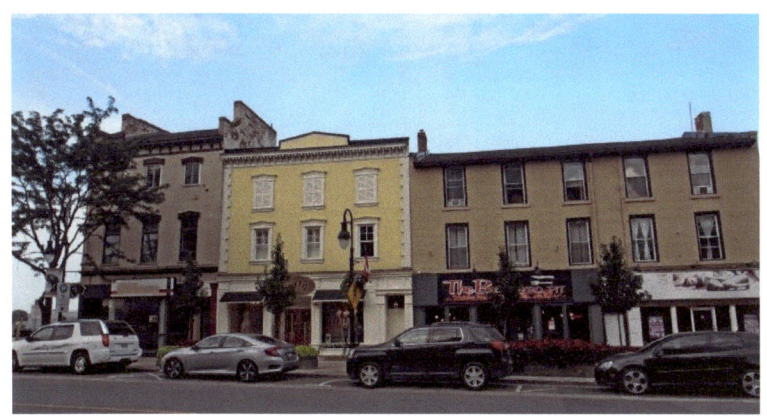

24 St. Paul Street – The Bull BBQ Pit

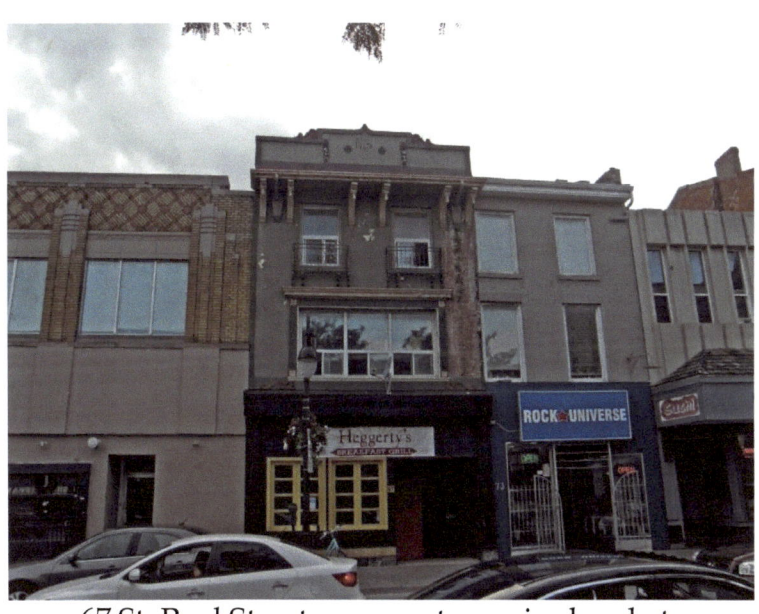

67 St. Paul Street – parapet, cornice brackets

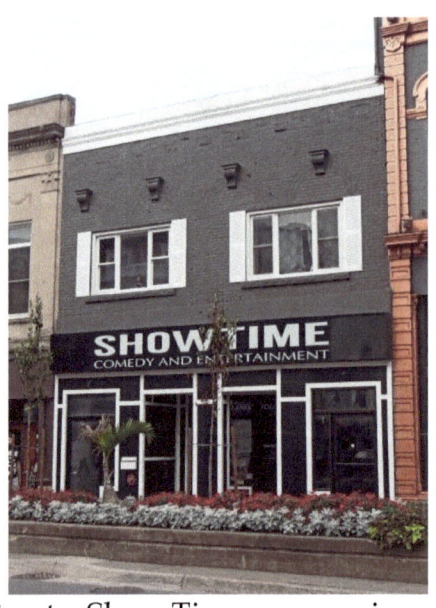

92 St. Paul Street – Show Time – voussoirs and keystones

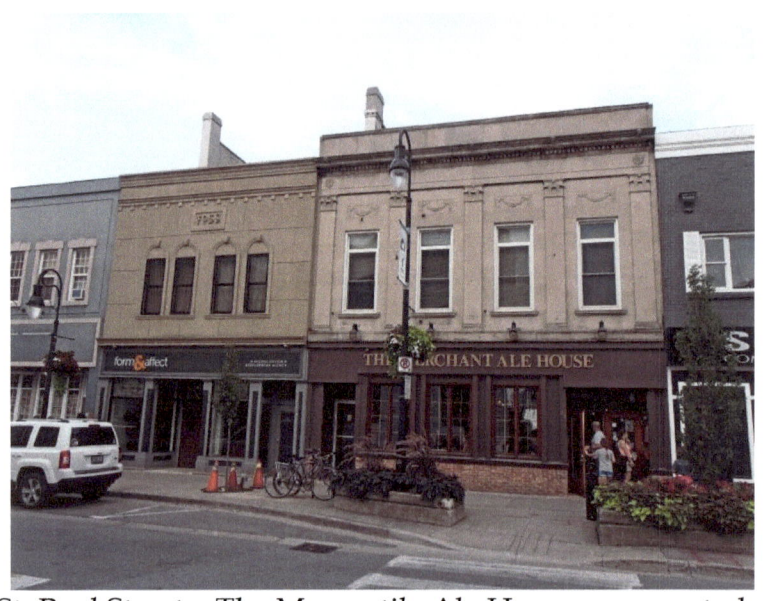

98 St. Paul Street – The Mercantile Ale House – parapet, dentil molding, pilasters, decorative brickwork above windows

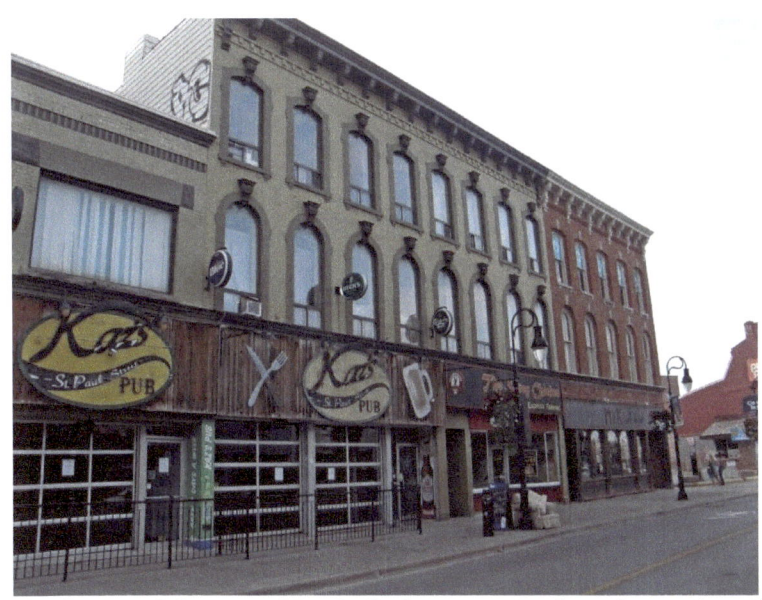

107 St. Paul Street – Kaz's Pub – cornice brackets, dentil molding, voussoirs and keystones

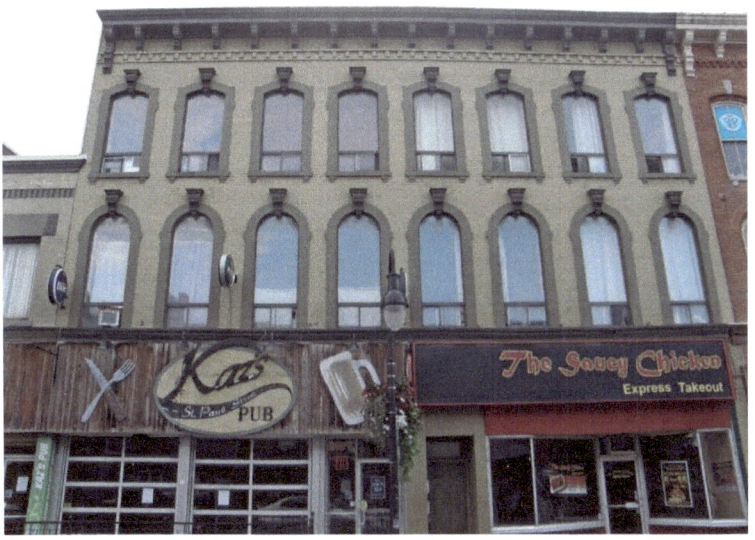

115 St. Paul Street – The Saucy Chicken

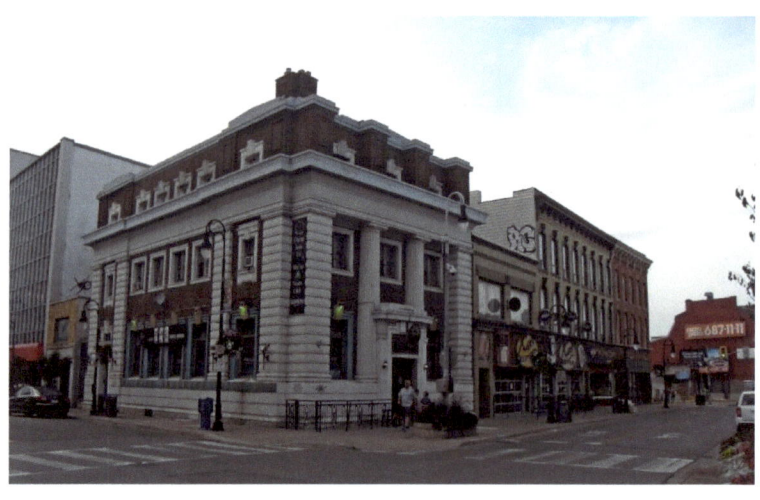

101 St. Paul Street – Patrick Sheehan's Irish Pub – parapet, keystones, engaged Doric pillars, pilasters

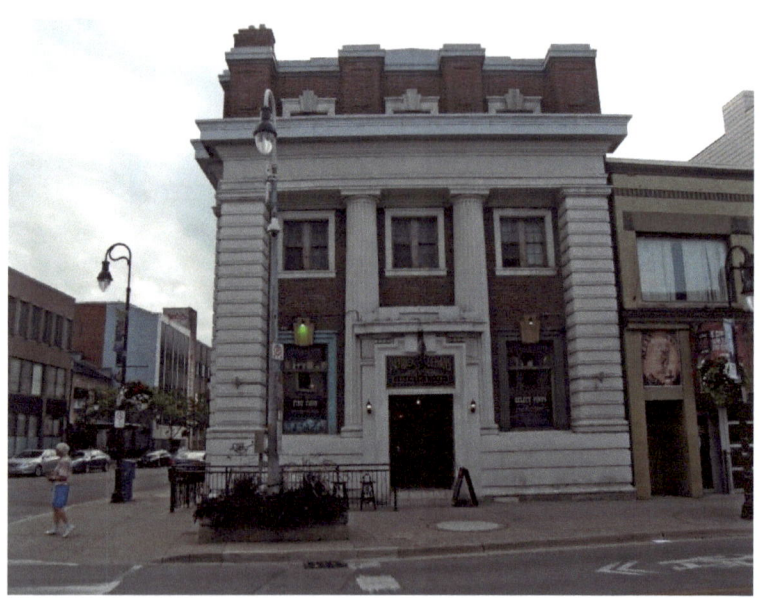

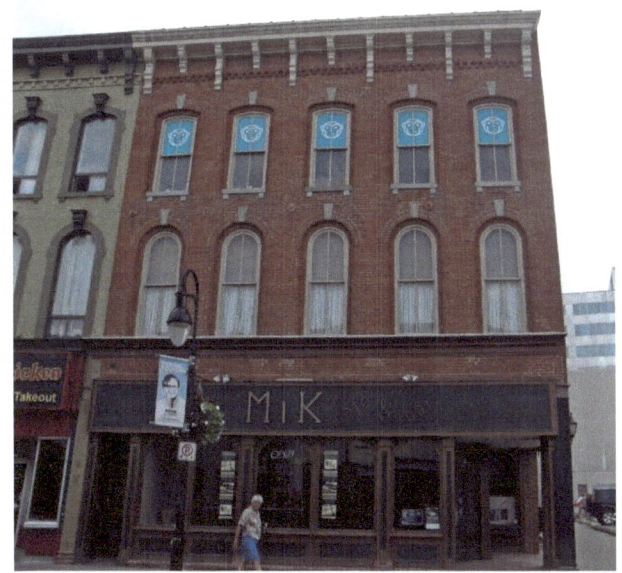

St. Paul Street – cornice brackets, voussoirs and keystones

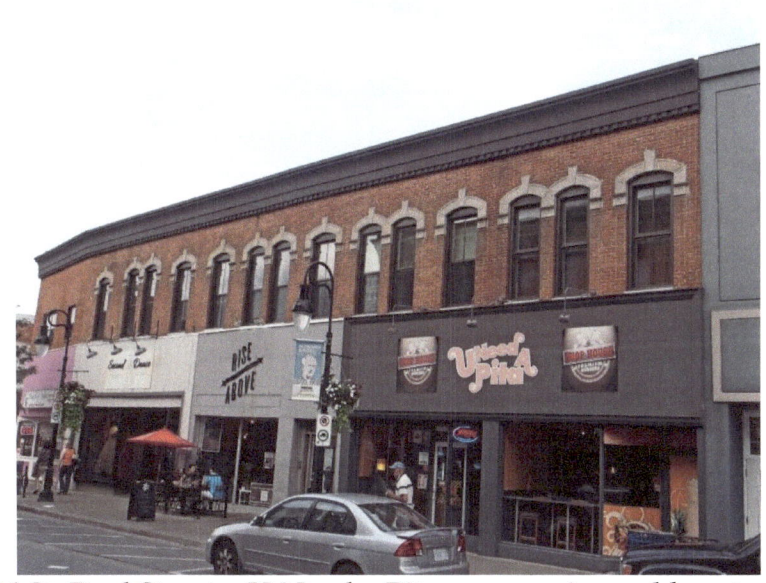

116 St. Paul Street – U Need a Pita – voussoirs and keystones

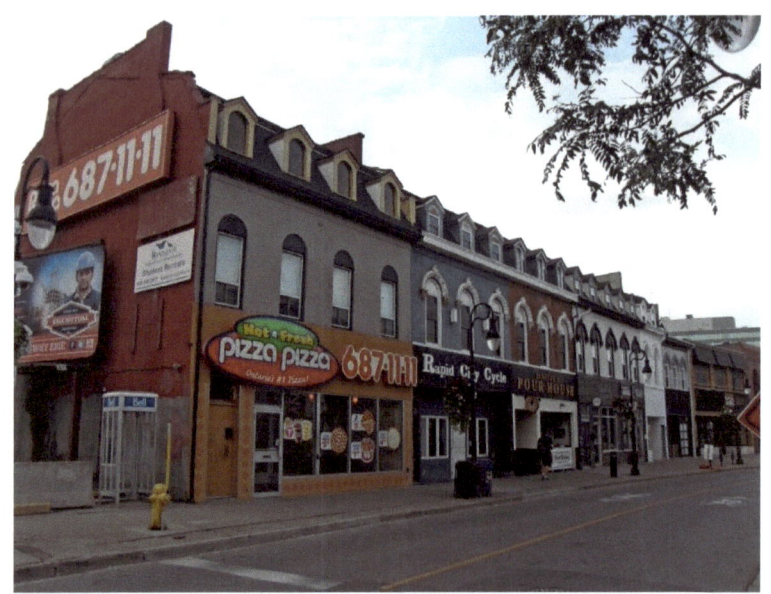

139 St. Paul Street – Pizza Pizza - dormers

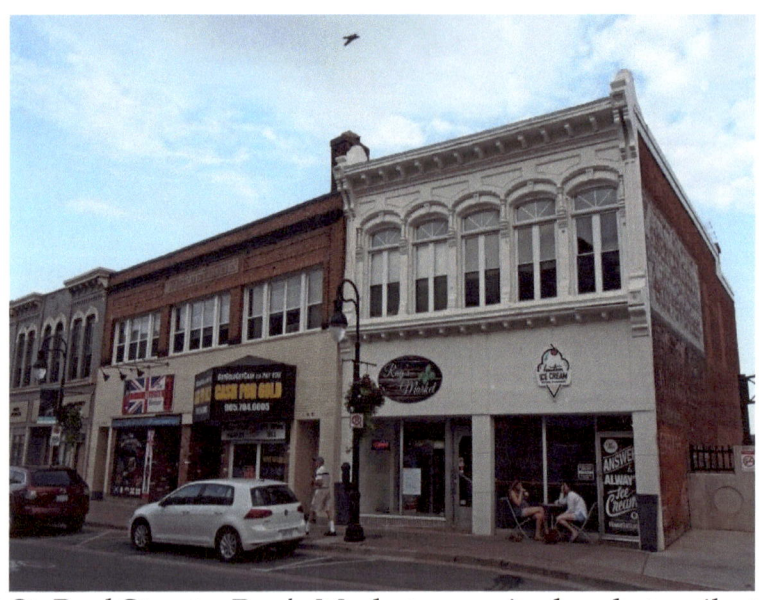

144 St. Paul Street – Ray's Market – cornice brackets, pilasters, fanlights above façade of five bays

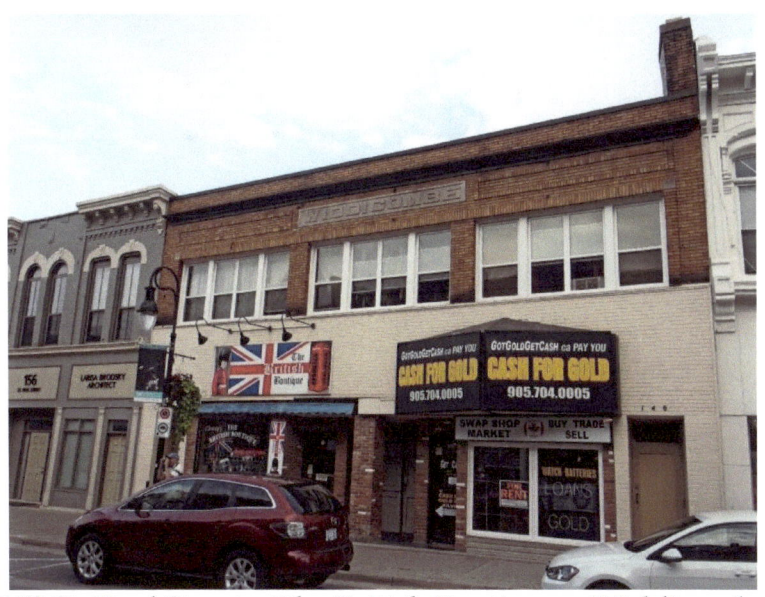

152 St. Paul Street – The British Boutique – Widdicombe Building

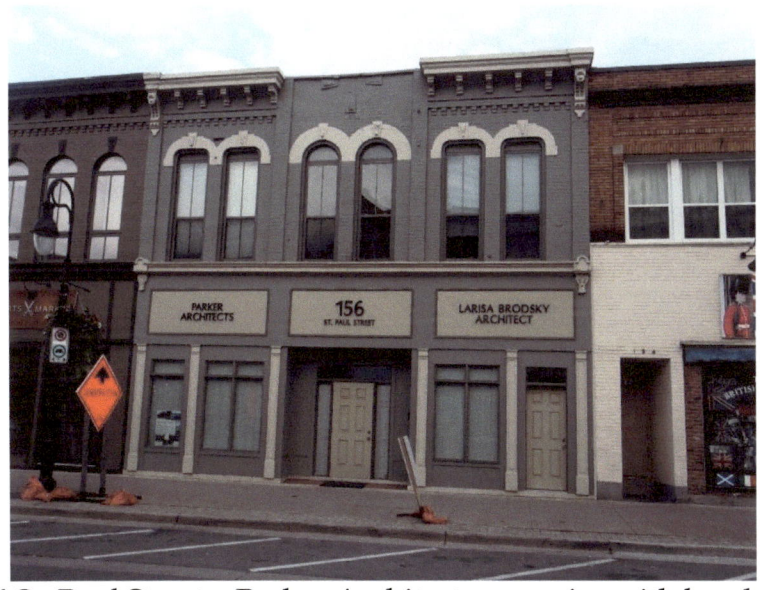

156 St. Paul Street – Parker Architects – cornice with brackets, dentil molding, voussoirs and keystones

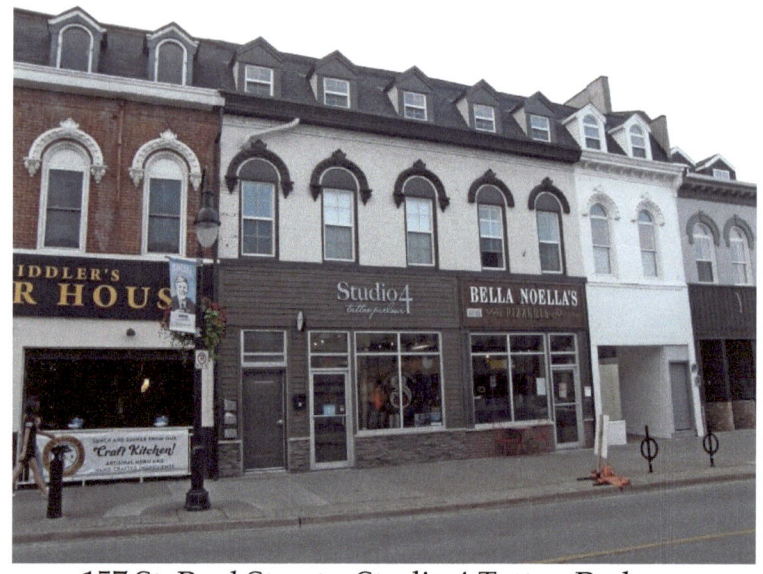

157 St. Paul Street – Studio 4 Tattoo Parlour;
159 St. Paul Street – Bella Noella's Pizzeria
Dormers, drip molds with keystones

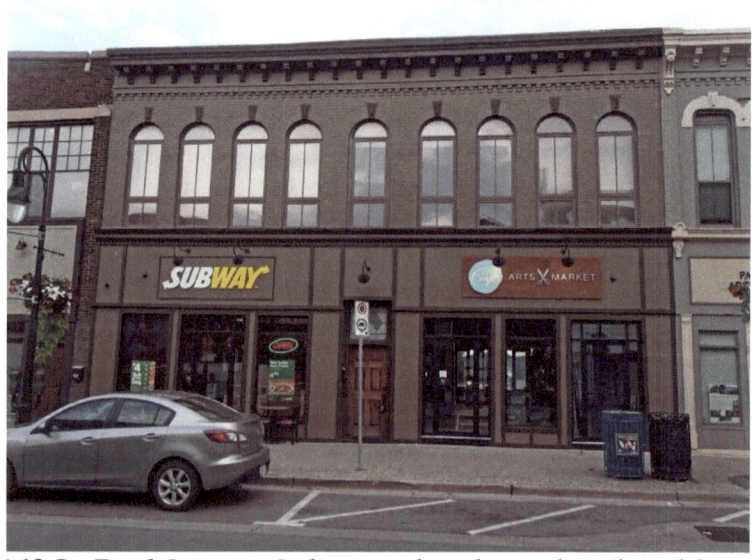

160 St. Paul Street – Subway – brackets, dentil molding, keystones

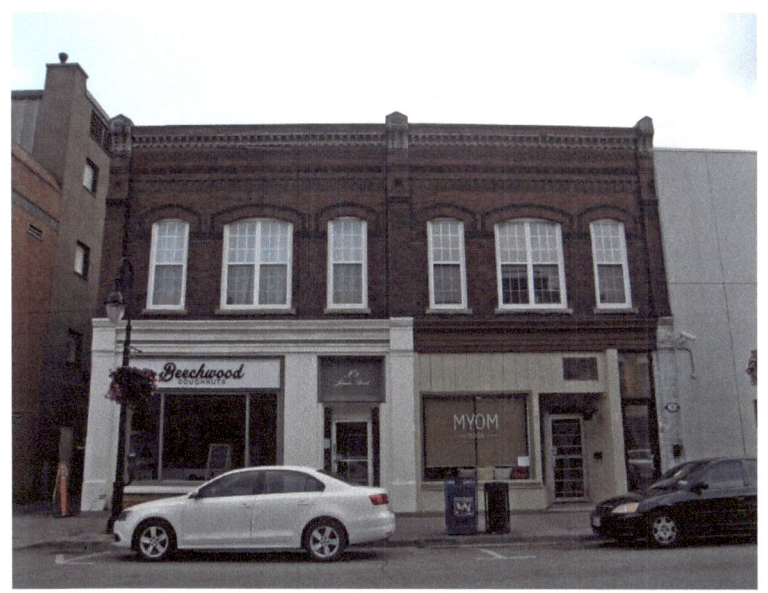

165 St. Paul Street – Beechwood Doughnuts – pilasters

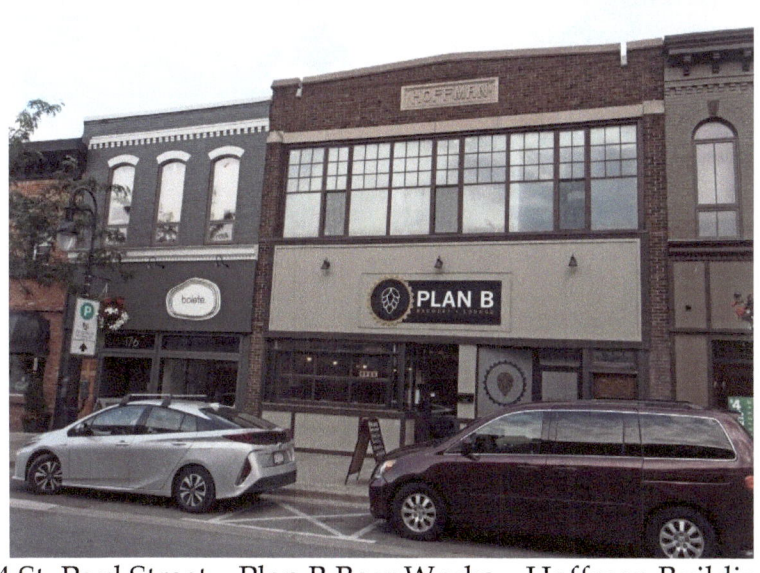

174 St. Paul Street – Plan B Beer Works – Hoffman Building – parapet

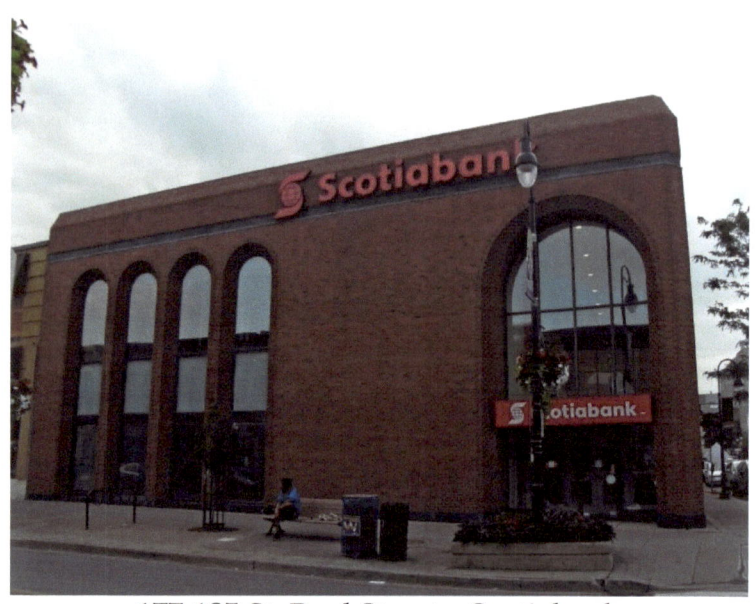

177-185 St. Paul Street – Scotiabank

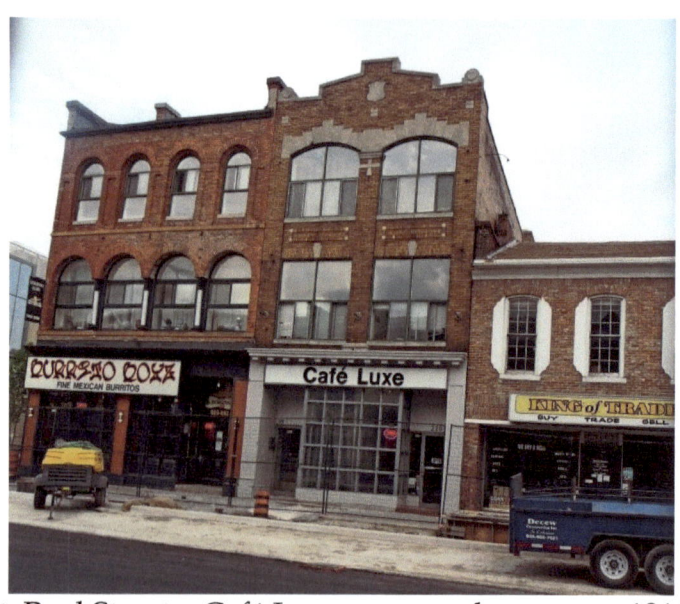

220 St. Paul Street – Café Luxe – stepped parapet – 1914 date stone, voussoirs, banding

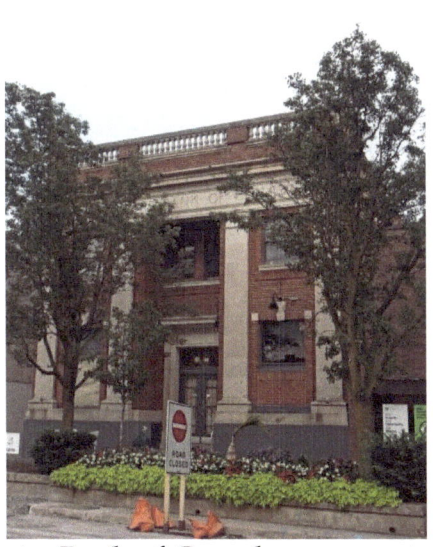

St. Paul Street – Bank of Canada – parapet with spindle balustrade, pilasters

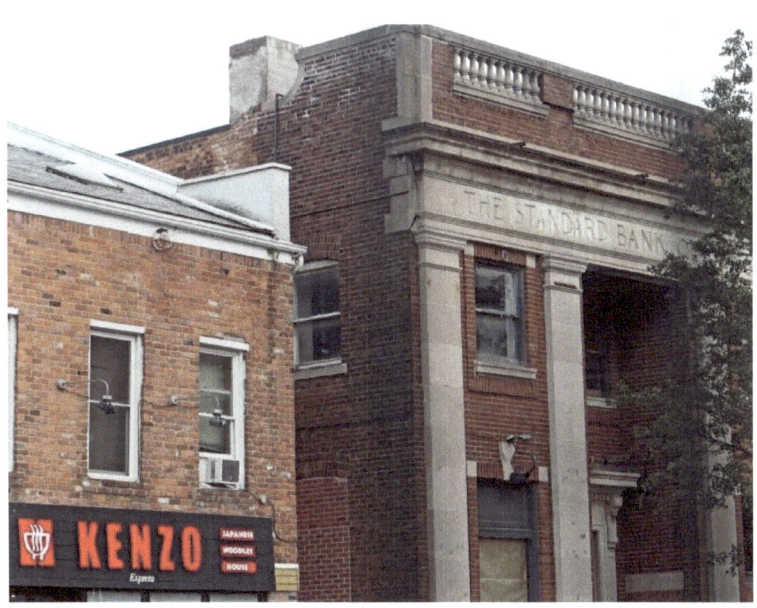

200 St. Paul Street – Kenzo Ramen

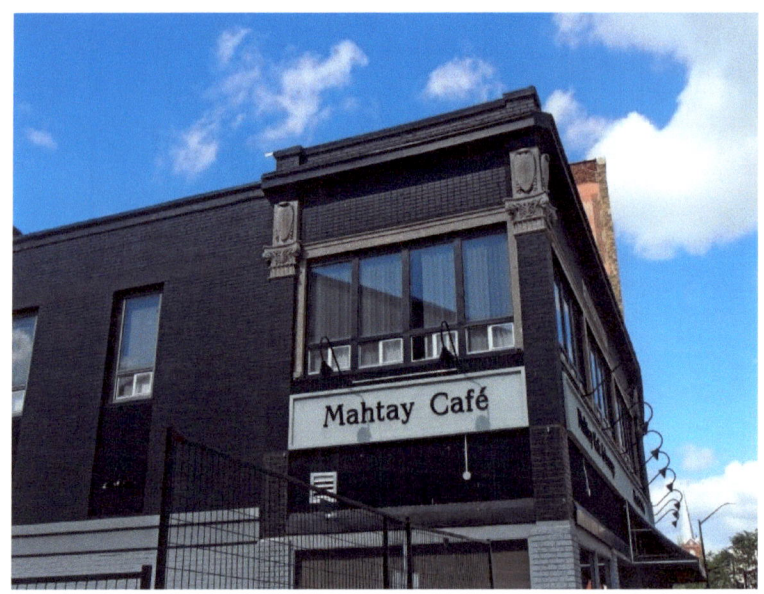

241 St. Paul Street – Maytay Café – pilasters with composite capitals each topped by a cartouche

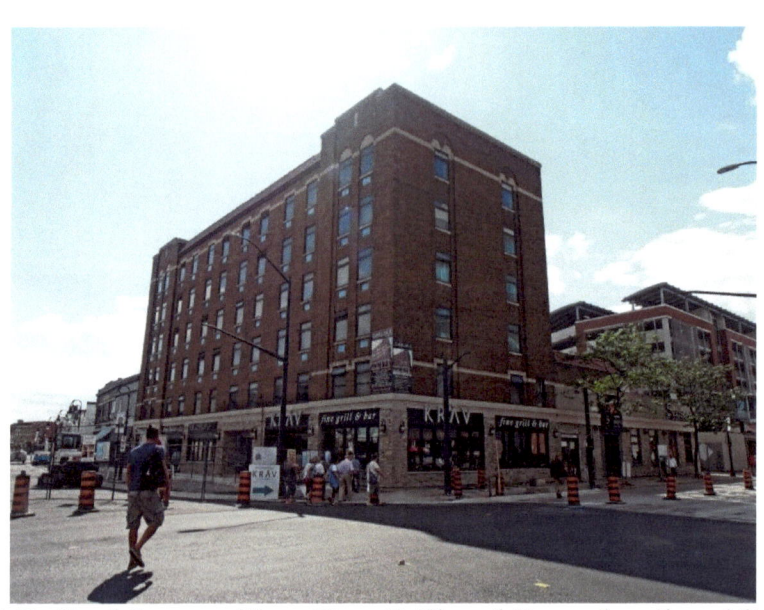

261 St. Paul Street – Krav Fine Grill and Bar – dentil molding, banding

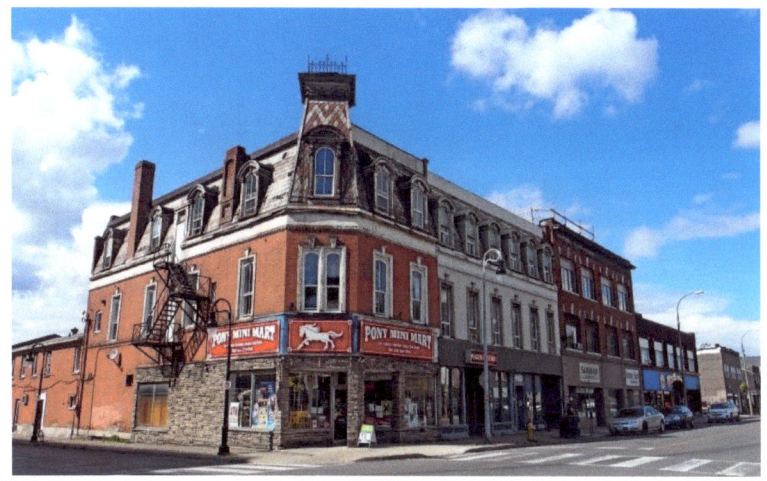

321 St. Paul Street – Pony Mini Mart – mansard roof with dormers, tower extending above roofline with iron cresting around widow's walk, trichromatic tile work, keystones

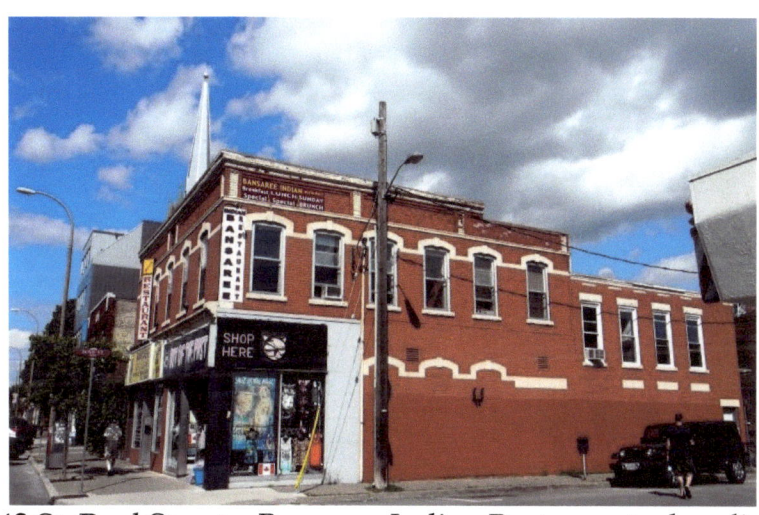

342 St. Paul Street – Bansaree Indian Restaurant – banding with keystones

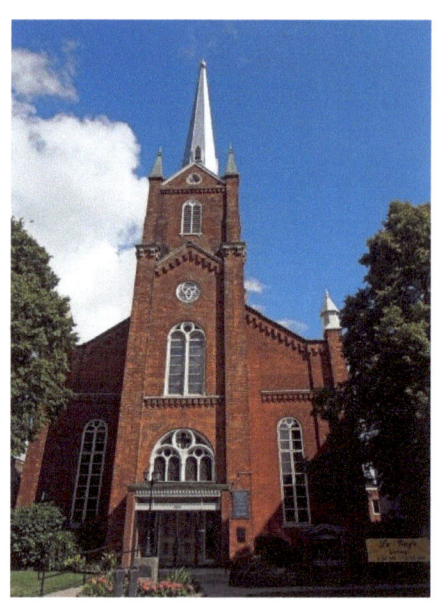

366 St. Paul Street – Silver Spire United Church came into existence on July 1, 2008, as an amalgamation of three former downtown St. Catharines churches: Memorial, St. Paul Street United and Welland Avenue.

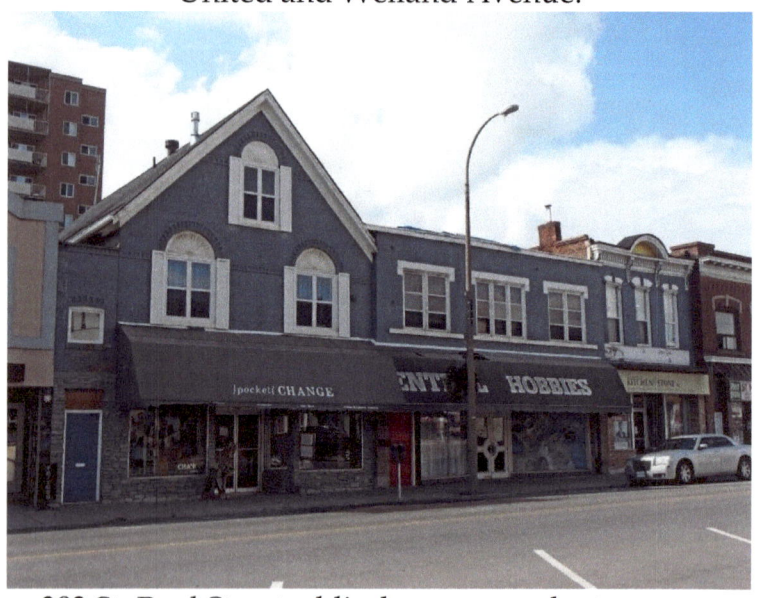

393 St. Paul Street – blind wagon-spoke transoms

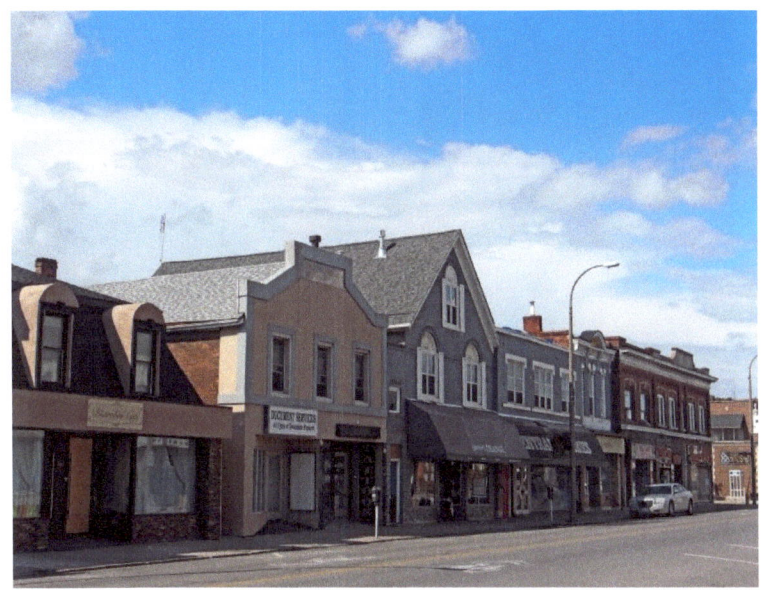

401 St. Paul Street – stepped parapet

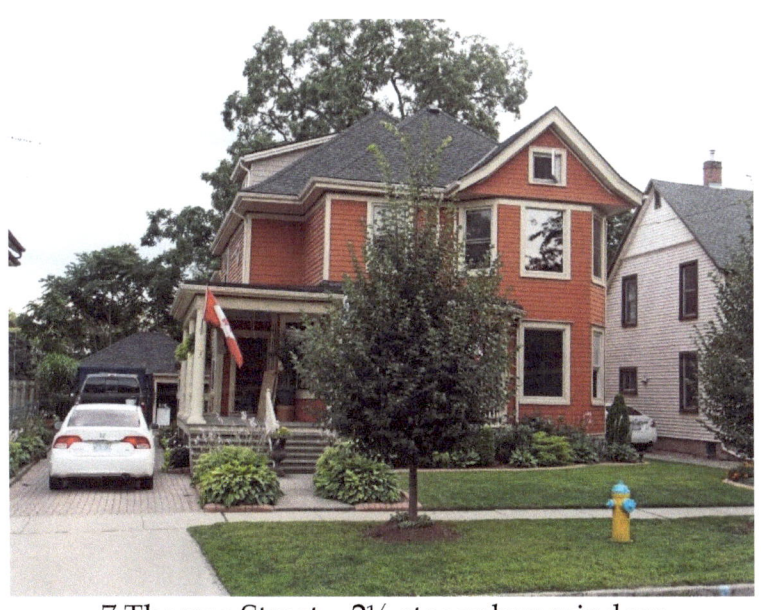

7 Thomas Street – 2½ storey bay window

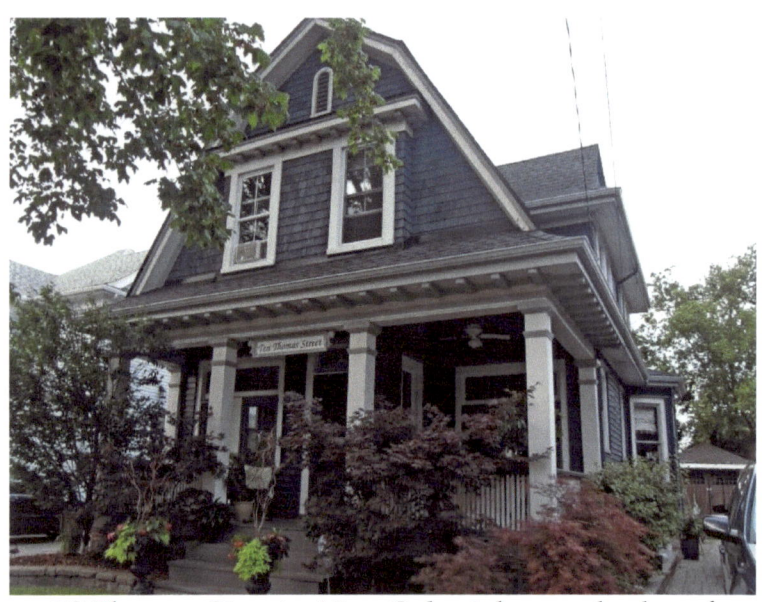

10 Thomas Street – Neo-Colonial – gambrel roof

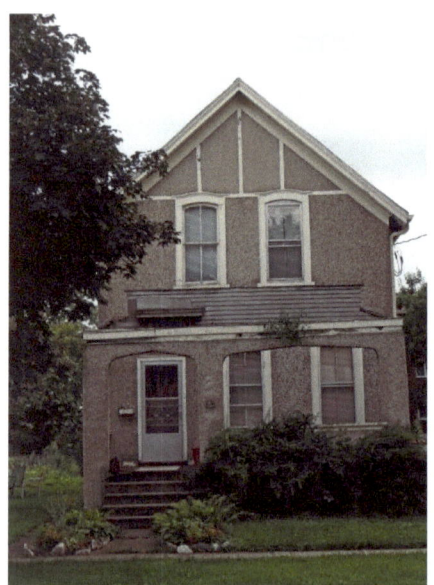

13½ Thomas Street
Tudor half-timbering on stucco

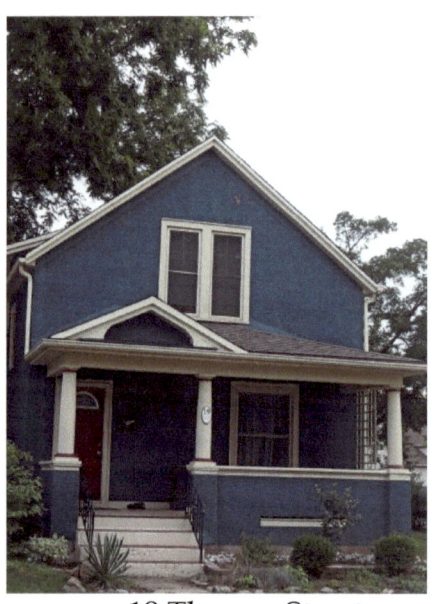

19 Thomas Street
Gothic, pediment

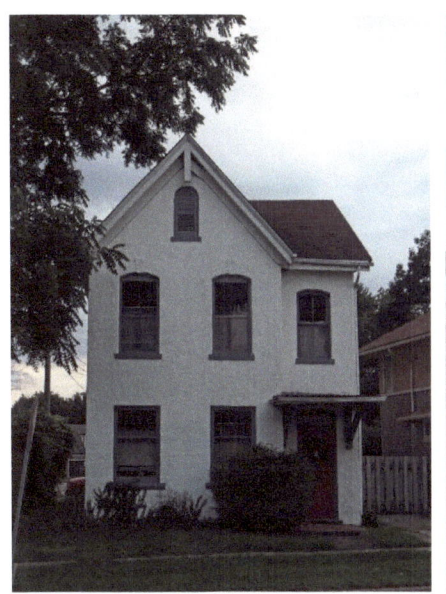

21 Thomas Street
Gothic – finial in gable

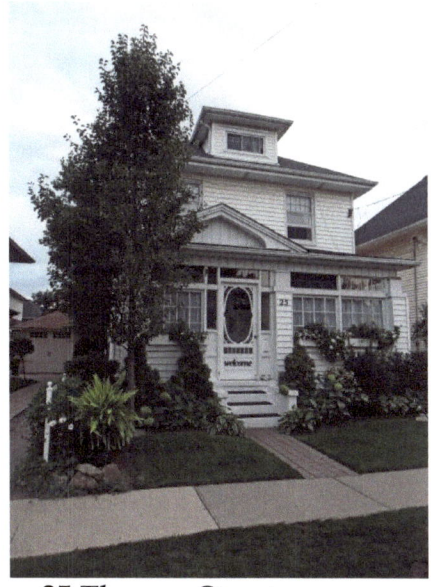

25 Thomas Street
dormer, pediment

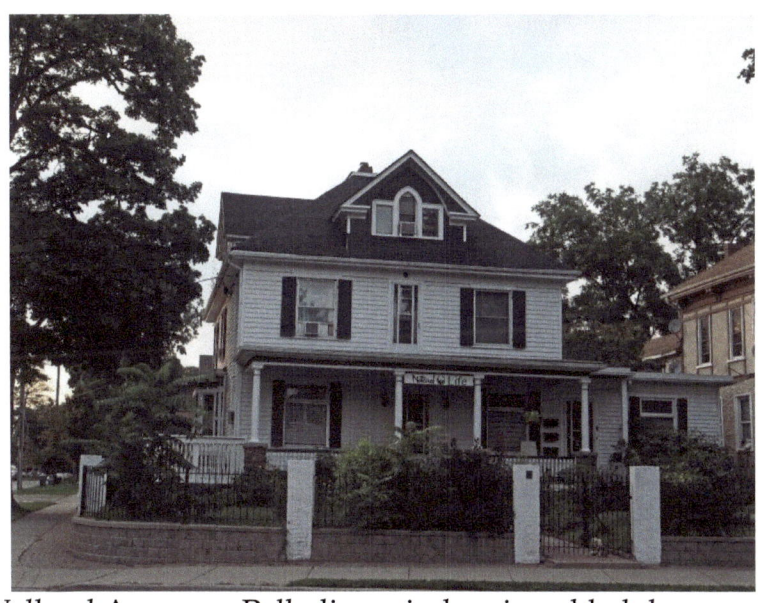

9 Welland Avenue – Palladian window in gabled dormer with cornice return

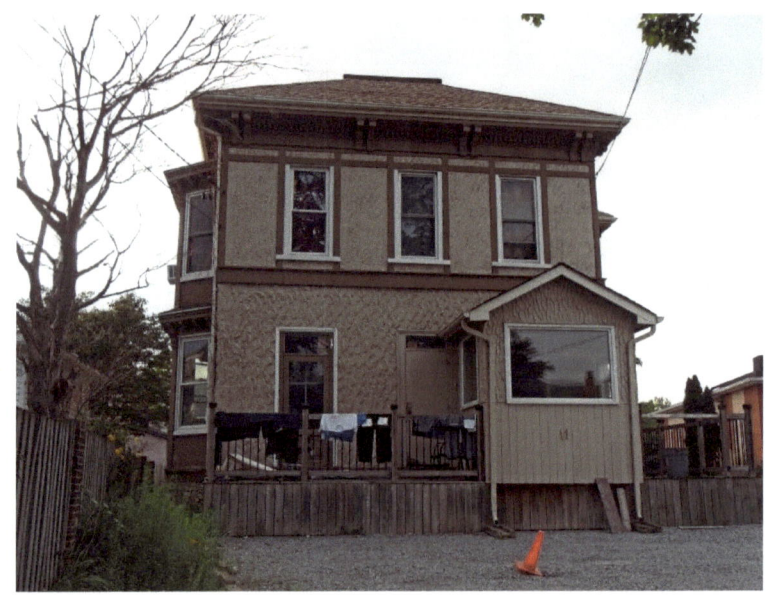

11 Welland Avenue – hipped roof, paired cornice brackets

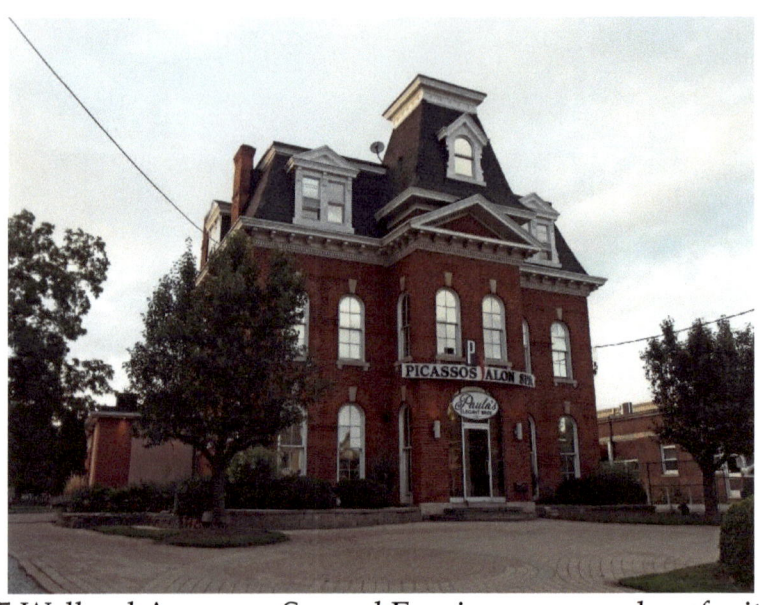

15 Welland Avenue – Second Empire – mansard roof with dormers with window hoods, three-storey tower, pediment, cornice brackets, voussoirs and keystones

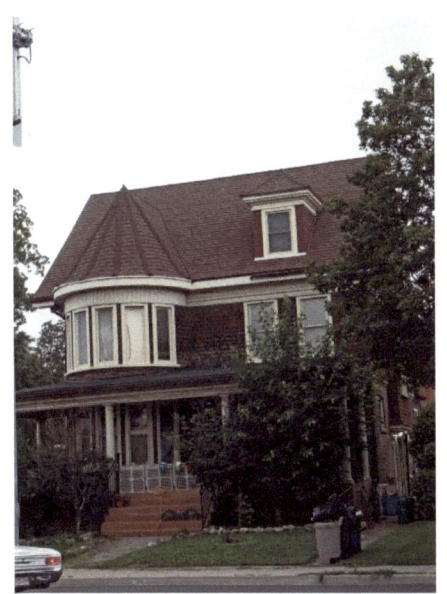

Welland Avenue – turret, dormer

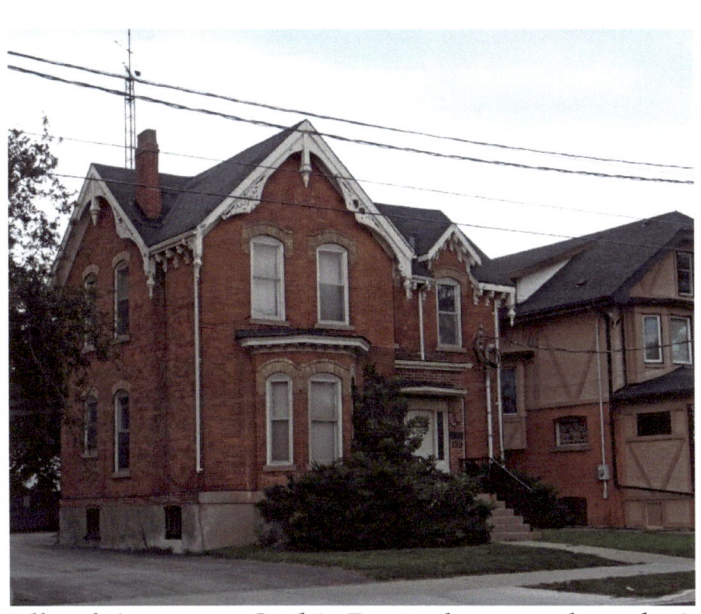

152 Welland Avenue – Gothic Revival – verge board trim and finial on gables, cornice brackets, voussoirs, bay window

Yates Street Heritage District

The Yates Street residential district was developed in the late 1800s and early 1900s along the banks of Twelve Mile Creek on land originally owned by William Hamilton Merritt. Soon after he moved to St. Catharines, Merritt began building a mill along the shores of the creek. There he discovered an artesian well with mineral water flowing from a deep cavity in the earth. This water could be boiled, leaving behind salt residue - a valuable commodity at the time. In later years, it was discovered that drinking or bathing in the mineral water could cure a variety of ailments. This prompted the development of two spa resorts on Yates Street - the Stephenson House and Springbank Hotel - allowing those with ailing health and vacationers from far and wide to test the healing powers of the mineral waters.

In the early to mid-1800s, many mills were constructed along Twelve Mile Creek, all of which needed a reliable source of water. The Erie Canal was being designed in the United States as a waterway that would divert vessels away from local businesses in Upper Canada. Hoping to solve both of these problems, Merritt formed the Welland Canal Company in 1824. The Company was made up of many investors, one of whom was John B. Yates, an entrepreneur from the United States. Yates Street was named in his honor. The Canal was finally finished in 1829, bringing vessels through Twelve Mile Creek on their way to the Great Lakes and beyond.

Many important businesses made their home on the banks of the Welland Canal. Yates Street was located very close to the new businesses so many of the mill owners and managers chose to reside there. They were generally very wealthy men and therefore wanted large, elegant homes. A lot of the homes were constructed in elaborate styles such as Georgian and Tudor that are rarely seen in other parts of the city due to the large size and detailing required.

Over the years, the home owners have wisely preserved many of the grown trees on their property, creating the beautiful tree-lined streetscape we see today. Although the mills and other canal side businesses ceased operation after a new route was chosen for the canal, the elegant residences remain, creating a beautiful eclectic neighborhood.

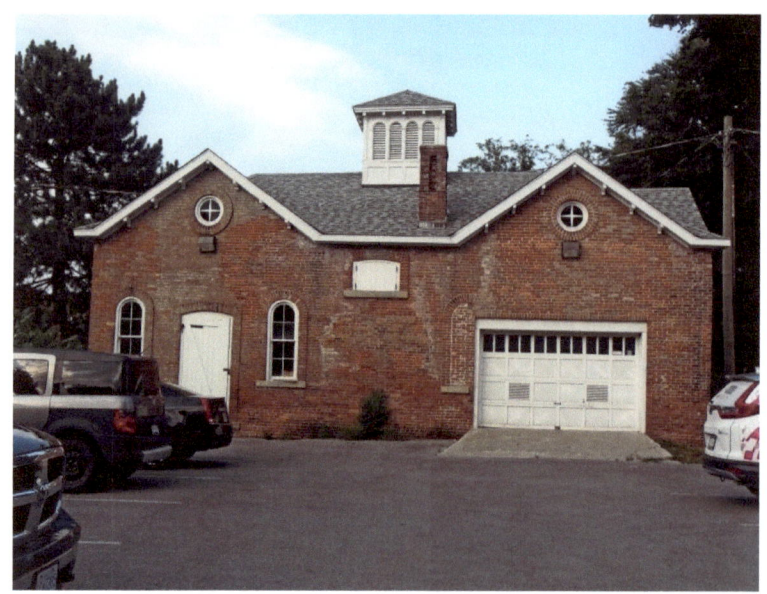
Yates Street – cupola

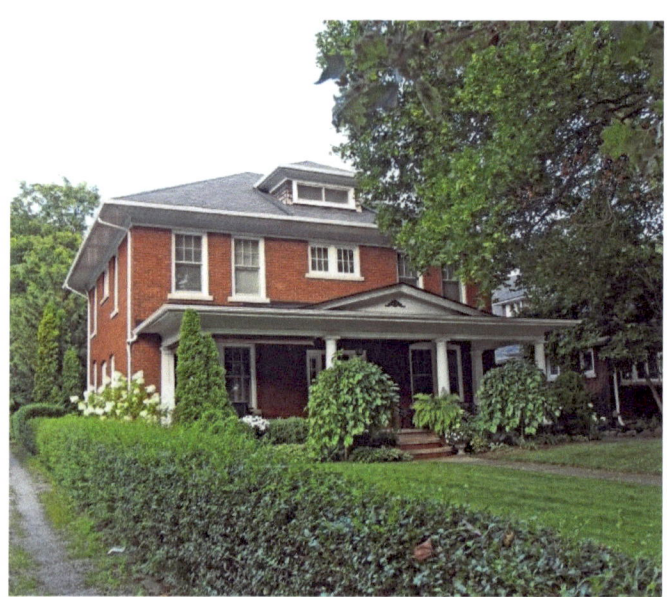
18 Yates Street – hipped roof, dormer, pediment

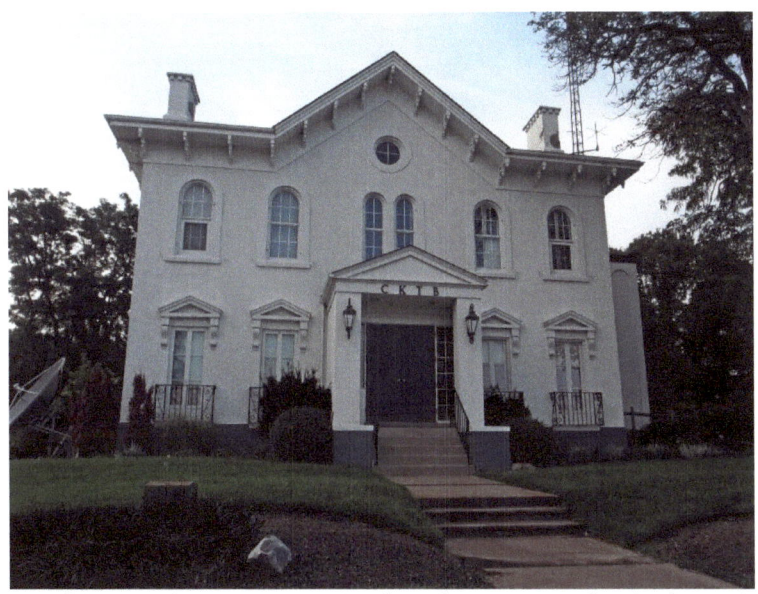

12 Yates Street – cornice brackets, round windows in gables, pedimented window hoods over lower windows, sidelights - Oak Hill was built in 1860 after Merritt's first house burned due to arson. Merritt was part of The Refugee Slaves Friends Society. The tunnels under Oak Hill house connected it to the coach house and another to Twelve Mile Creek. There was plenty of space to hide escaping slaves, and it was an important stop on the Underground Railway. In 1938 the building was converted into CKTB radio station.

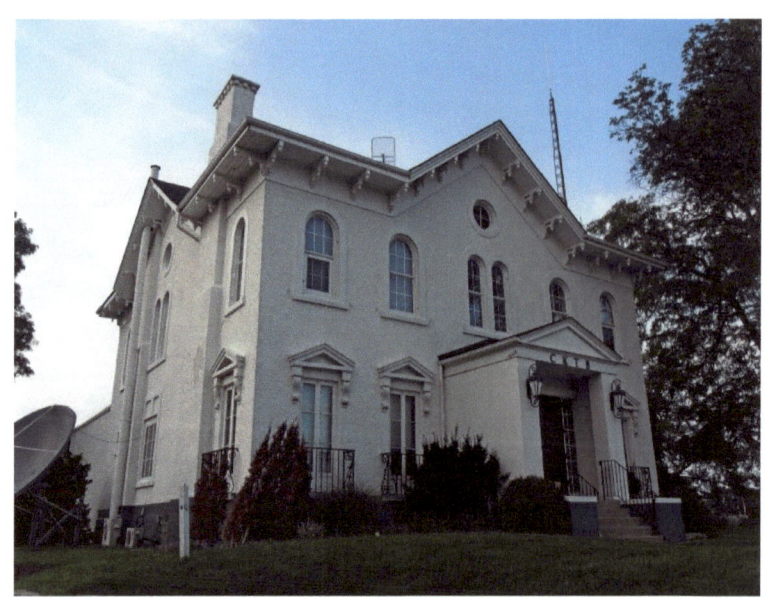

12 Yates Street

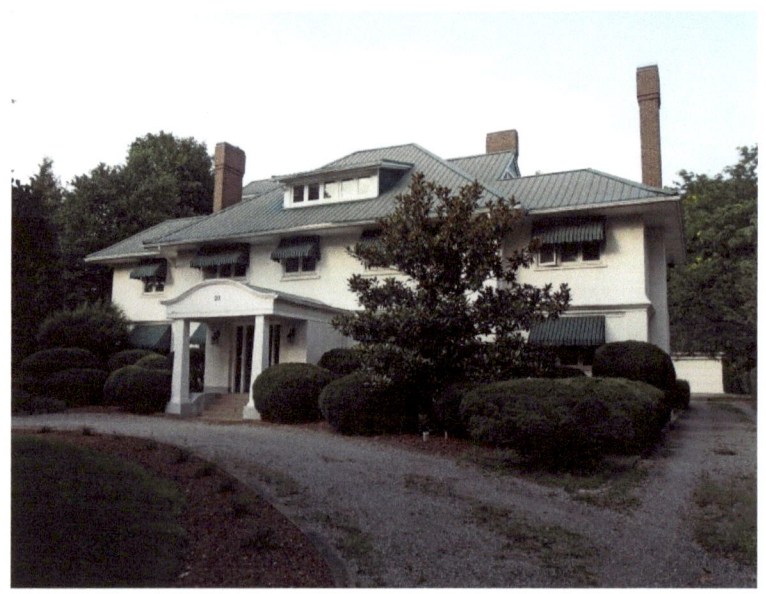

20 Yates Street – dormer in attic

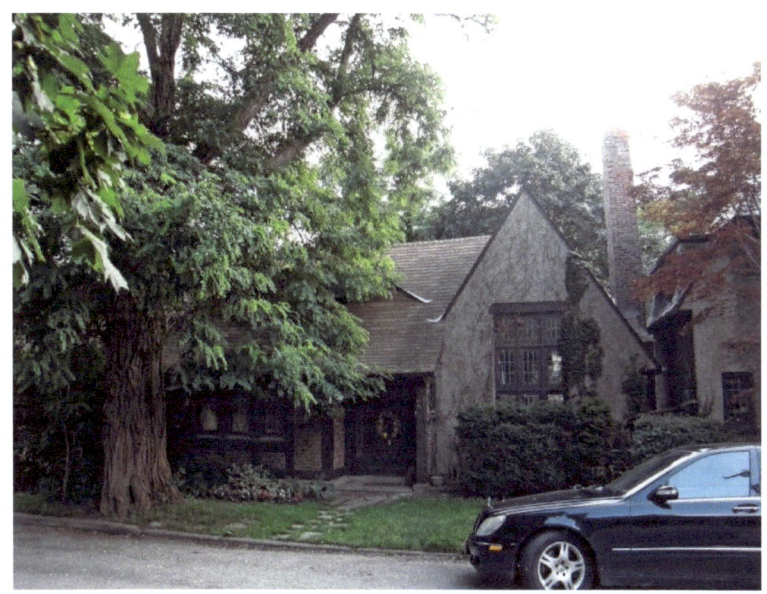

21 Yates Street

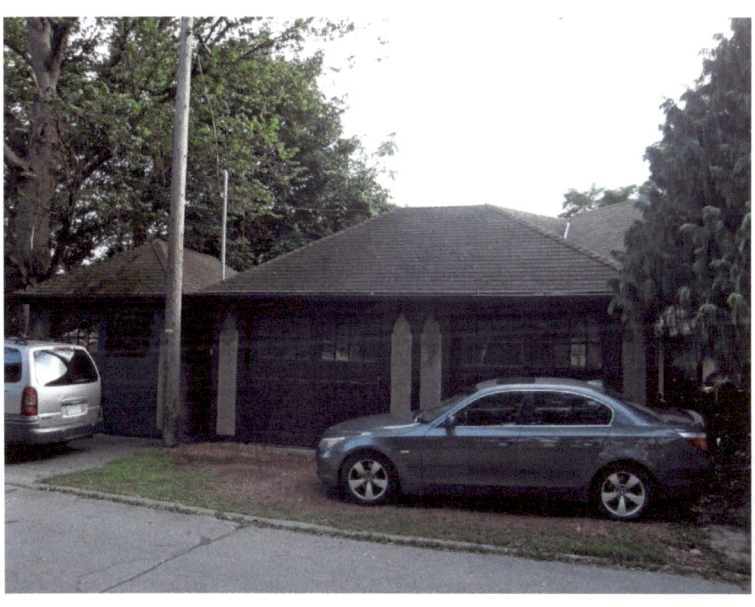

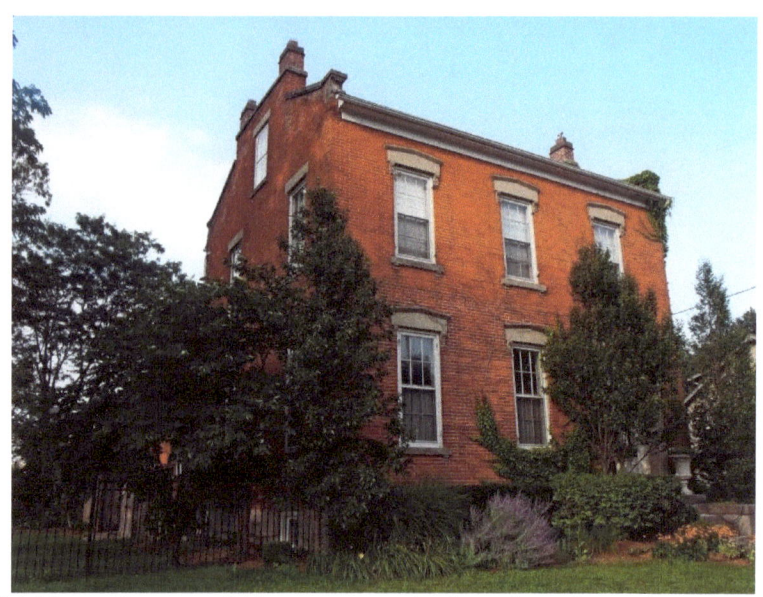

24 Yates Street – 2½ storeys, window hoods with cornice brackets

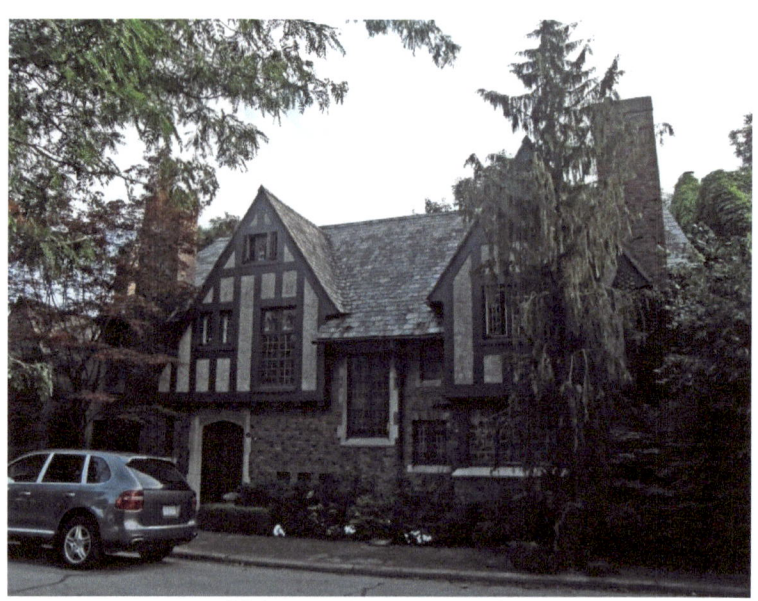

23 Yates Street - Tudor

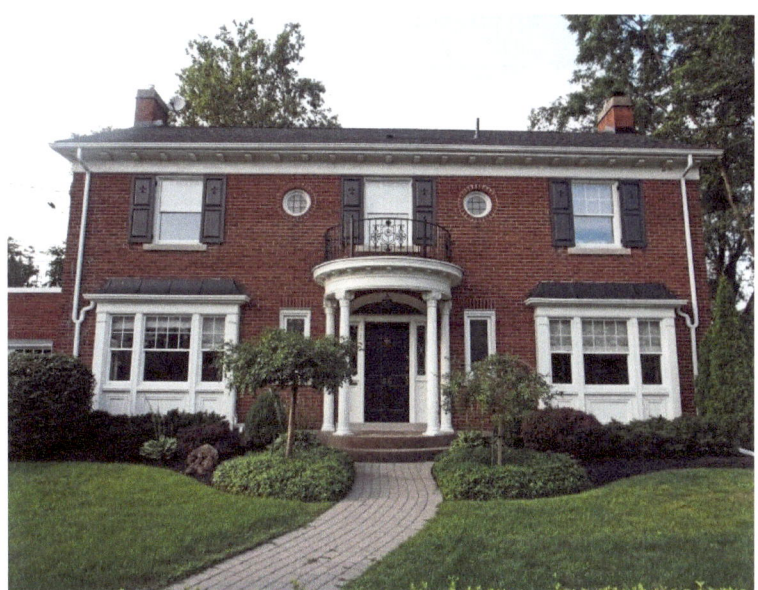

26 Yates Street – Classical Revival – second floor semi-circular balcony above pillared porch with composite capitals, sidelights and transom

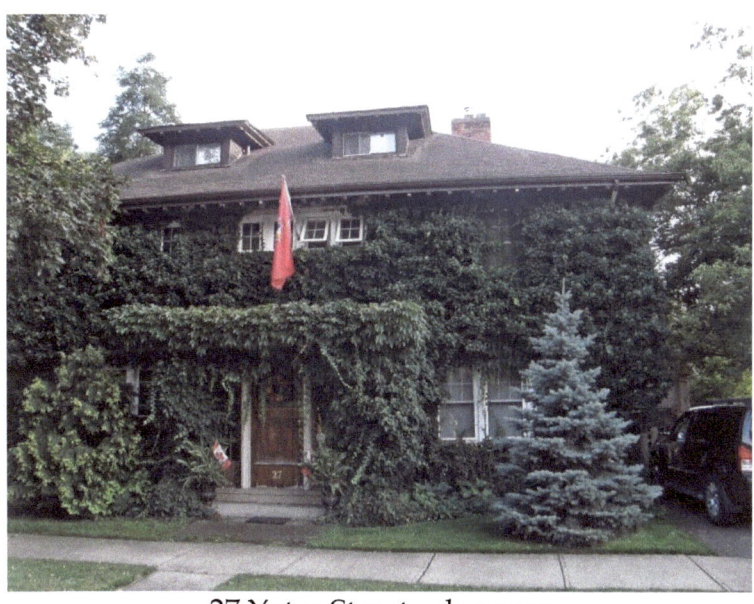

27 Yates Street - dormers

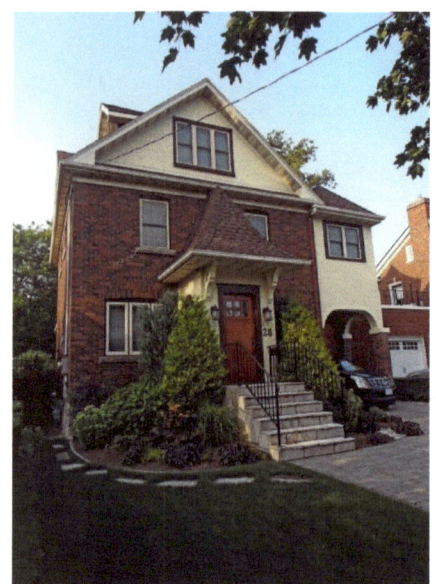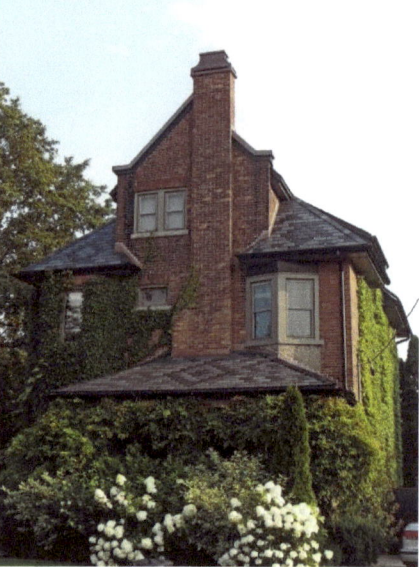

28 Yates Street - Edwardian

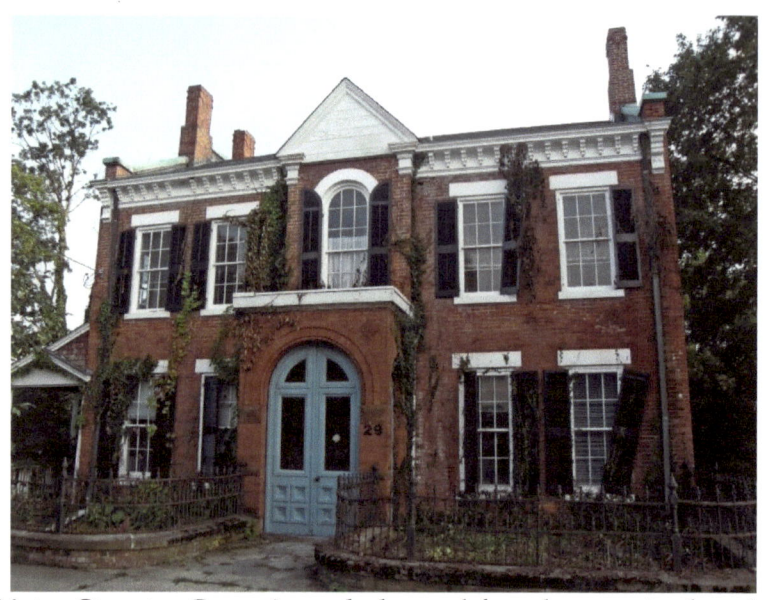

29 Yates Street – Georgian – balanced façade, cornice brackets, shutters on six-over-six windows

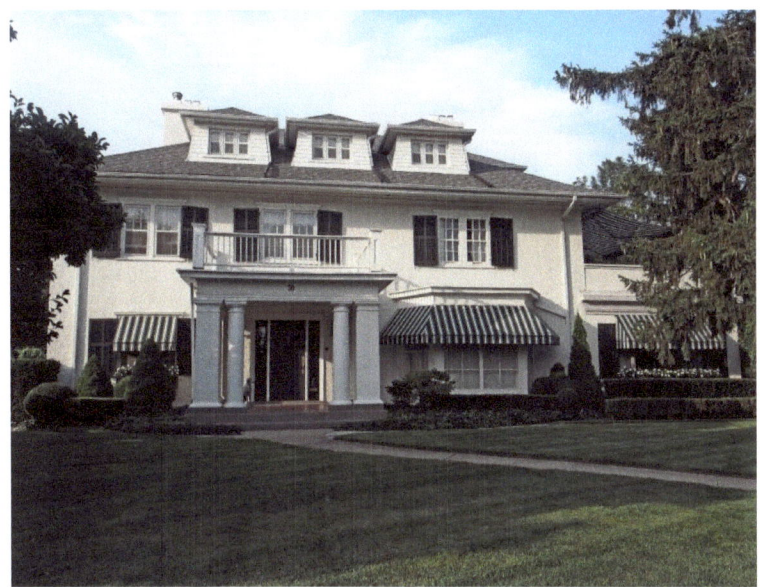

30 Yates Street – three dormers, second floor balcony above pillared entrance with sidelights, bay window

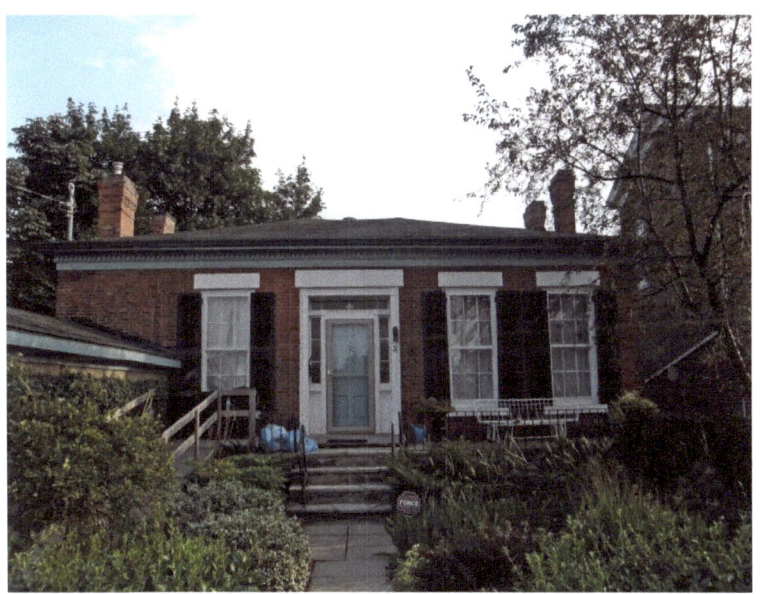

31 Yates Street – Regency Cottage, sidelights and transom

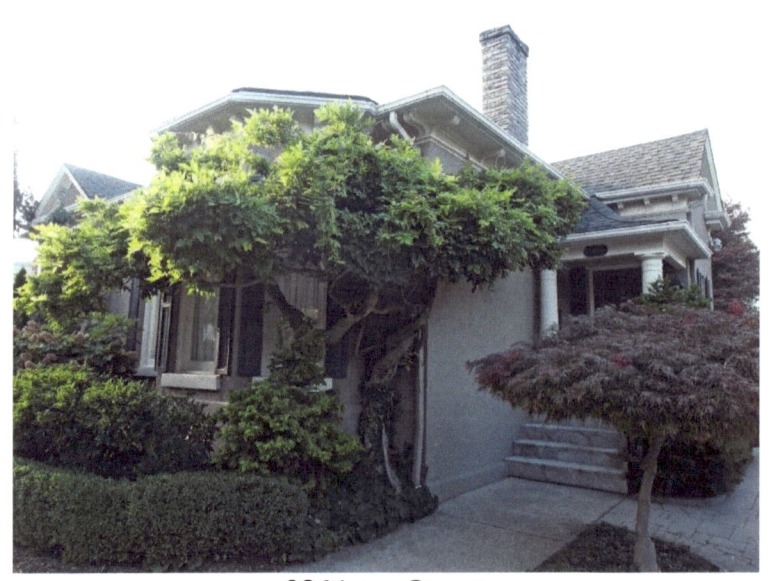

32 Yates Street

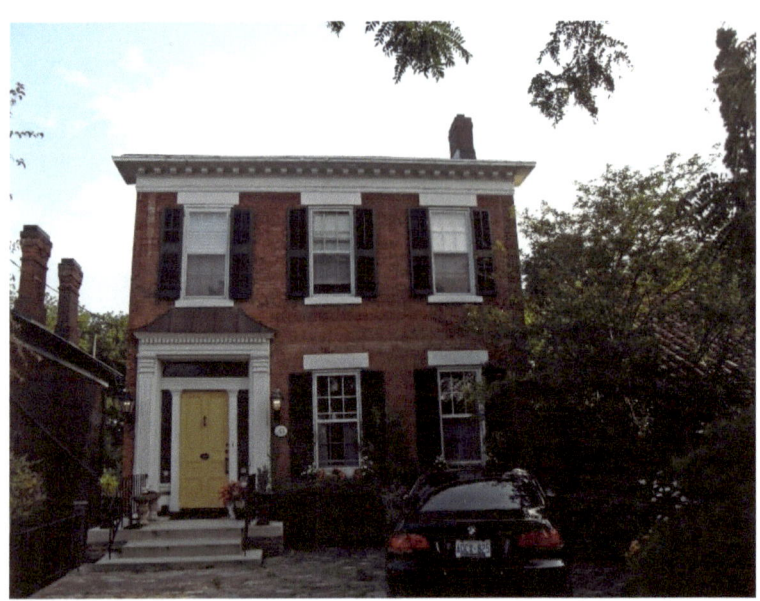

33 Yates Street – hipped roof, cornice brackets, shutters, engaged pillars around door with sidelights and transom

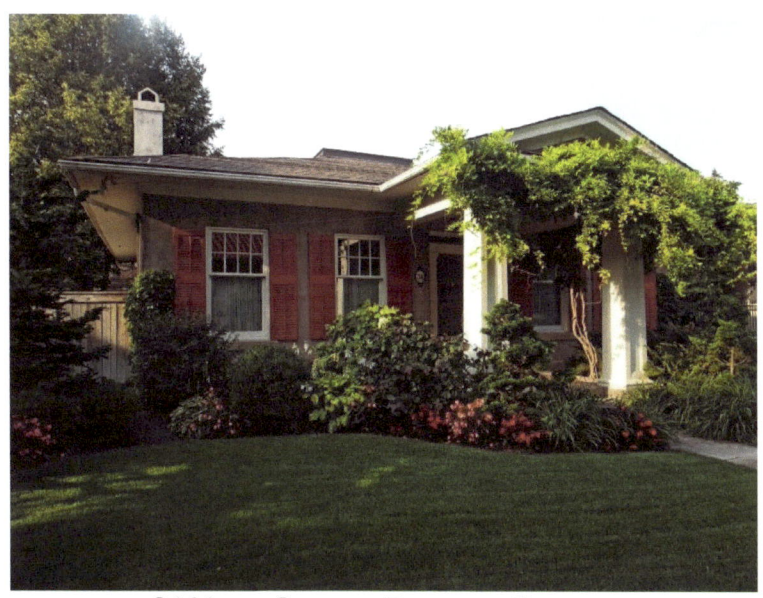

34 Yates Street – Regency Cottage

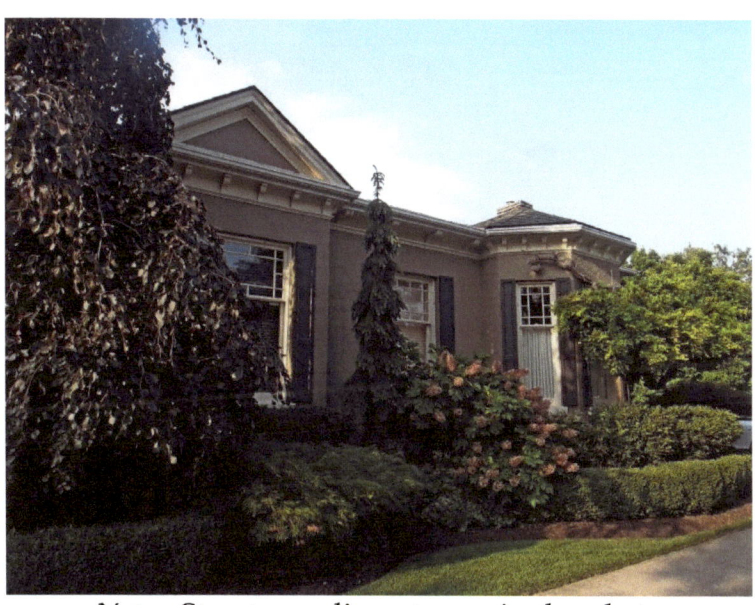

Yates Street – pediment, cornice brackets

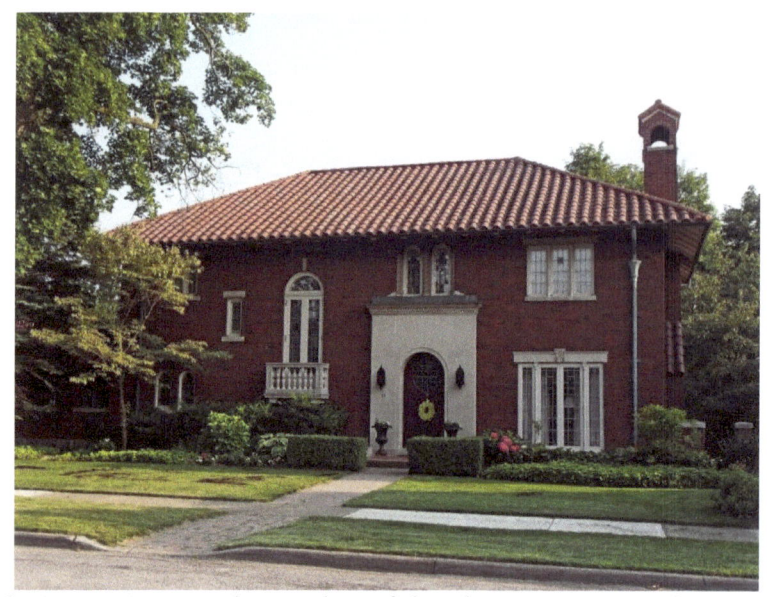

35 Yates Street – hipped roof, brick voussoirs with stone keystones, raised balcony with spindle railing

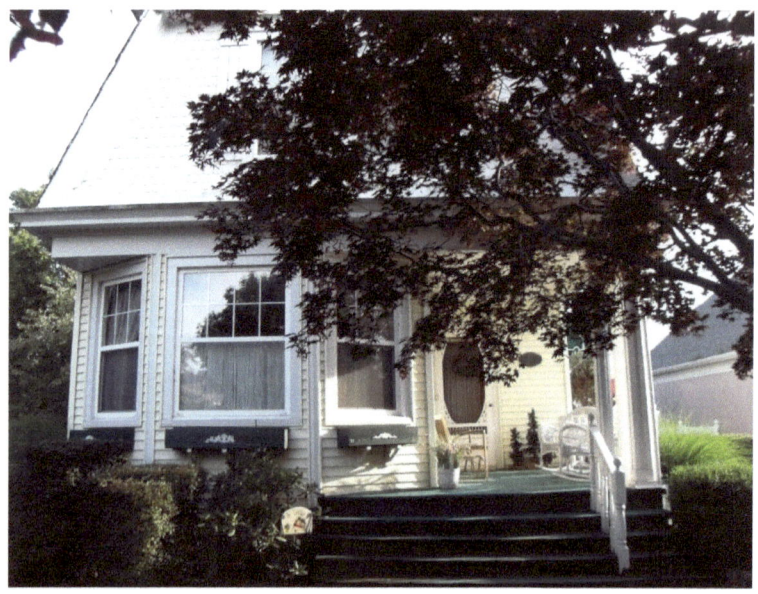

37 Yates Street

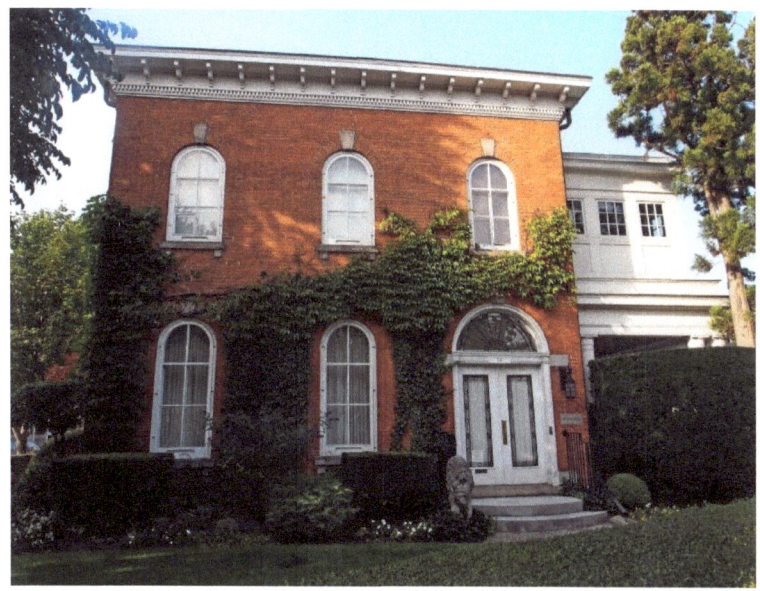

38 Yates Street – cornice brackets, voussoirs and keystones above semi-circular windows, door with transom window

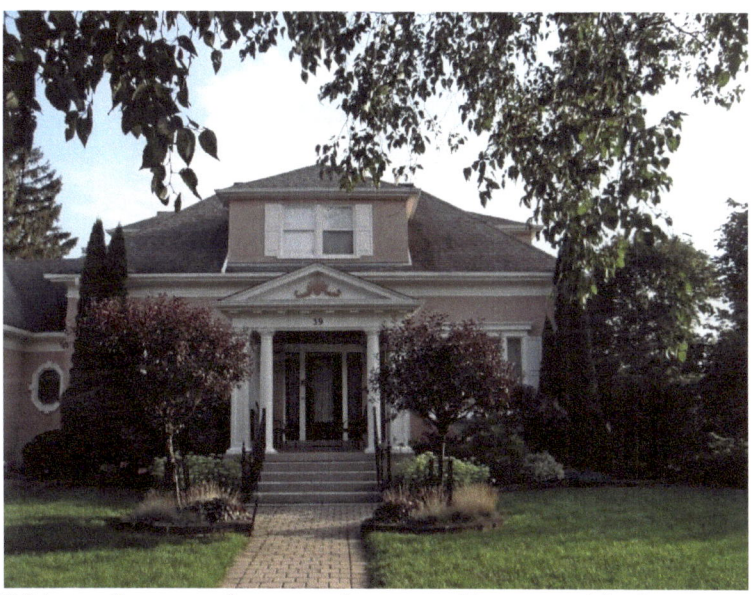

39 Yates Street – dormer above pediment with decorated tympanum above pillared porch, sidelights and transom

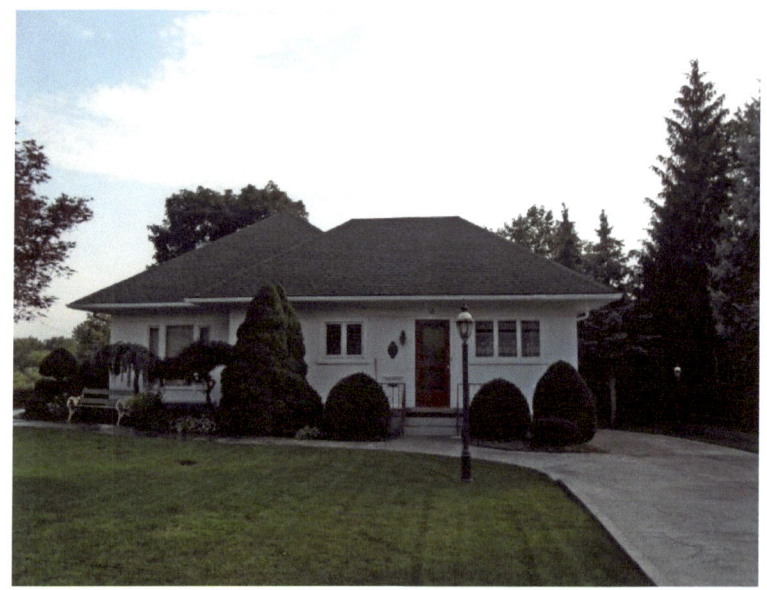

41 Yates Street – hipped roofs

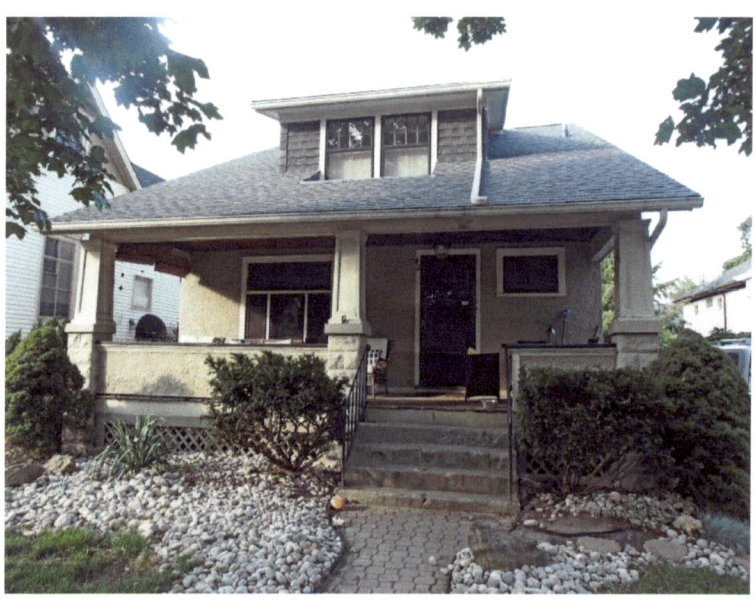

Yates Street – dormer in attic

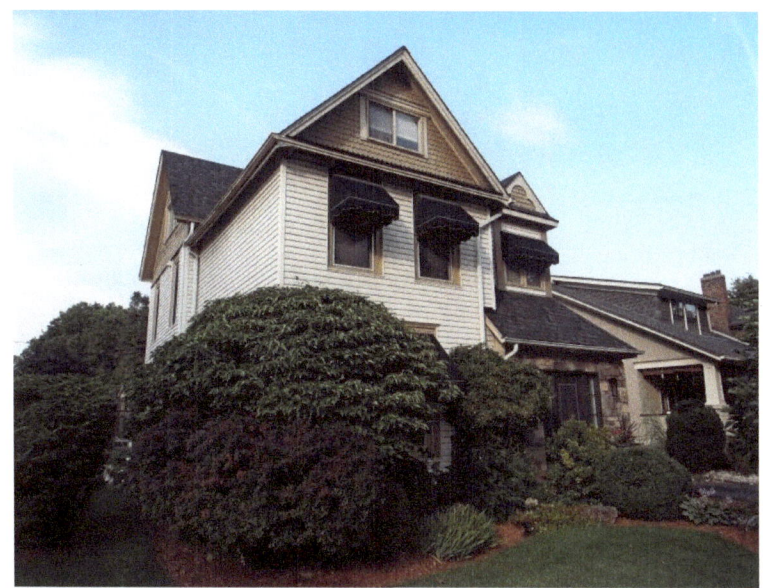

Yates Street

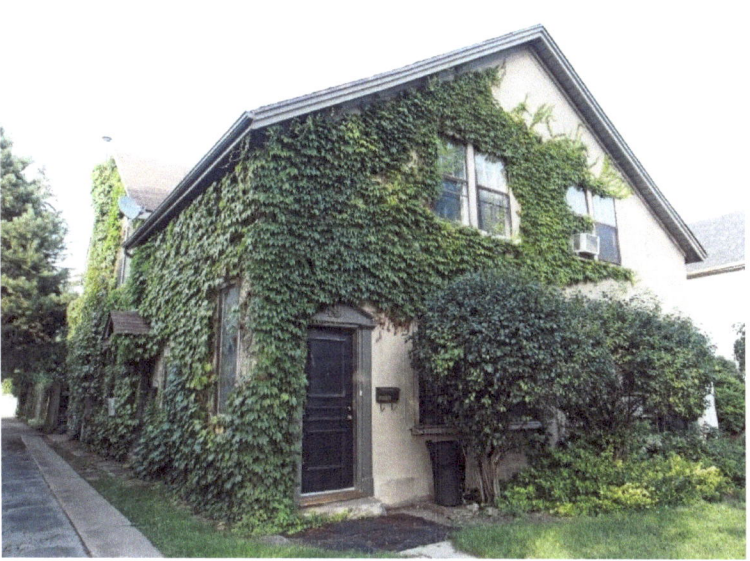

Yates Street

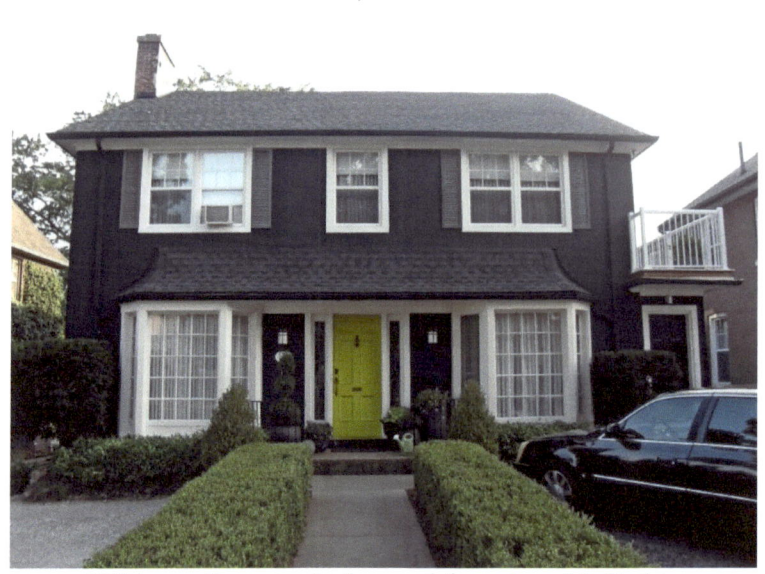

47 Yates Street – balanced façade, sidelights

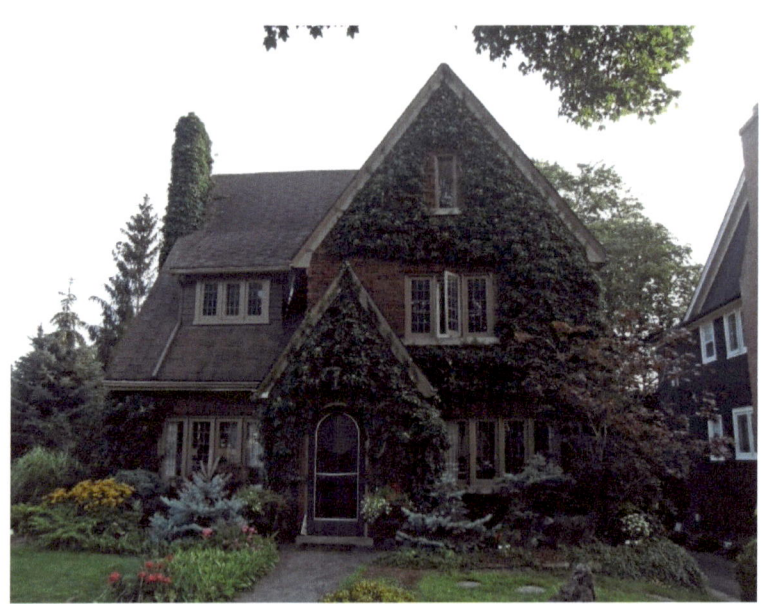

Yates Street

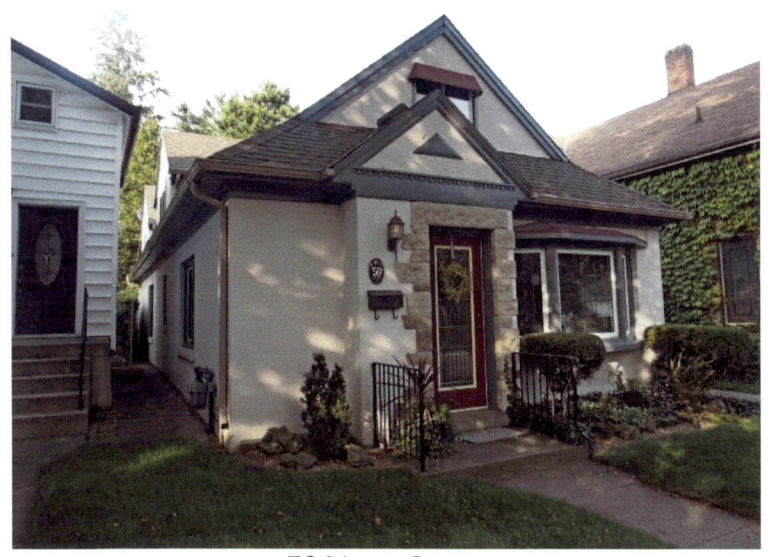

50 Yates Street

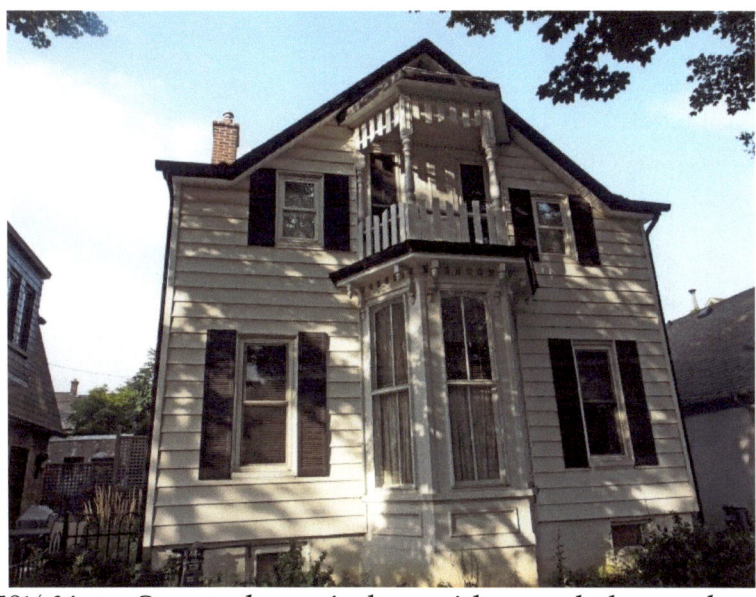

50½ Yates Street – bay window with open balcony above

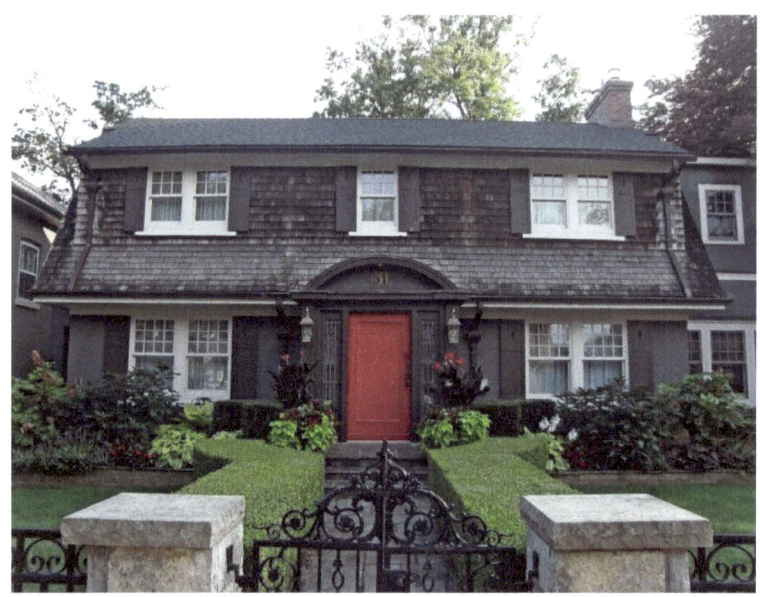

51 Yates Street – shed dormer across width of house, semi-circular pediment above door with sidelights

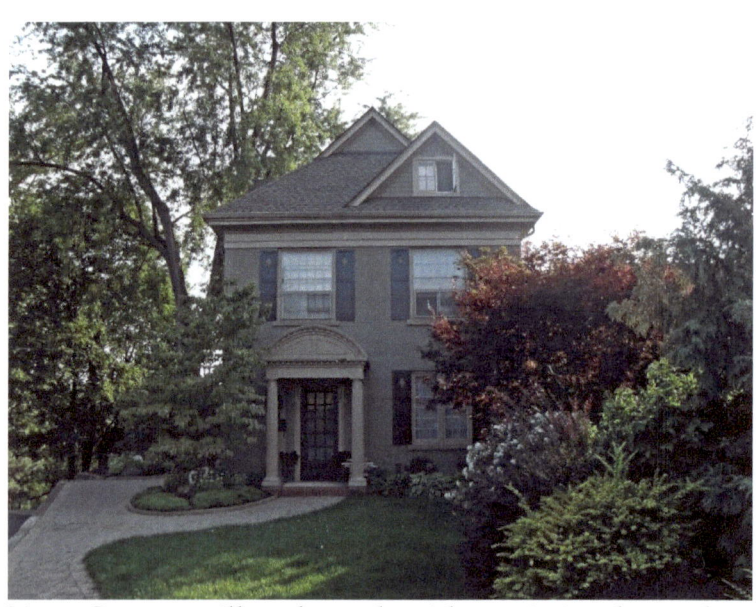

52 Yates Street – pillared porch with semi-circular pediment above door

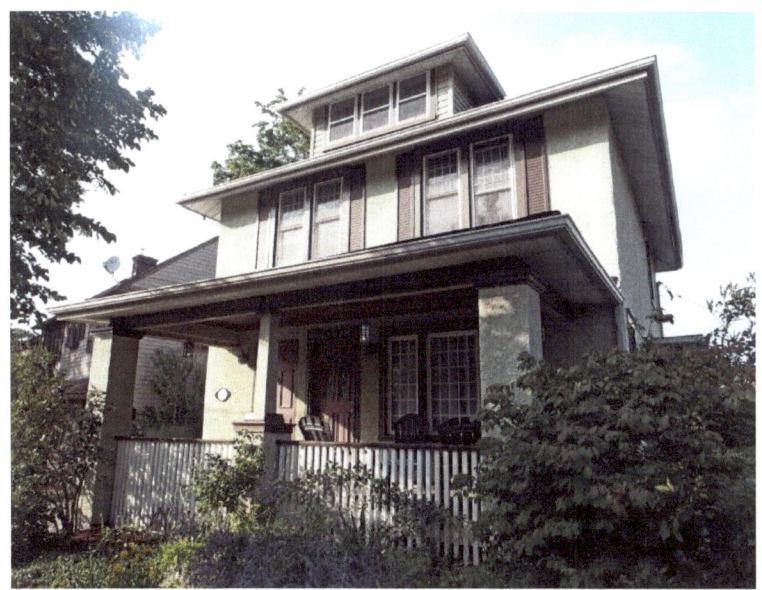

54 Yates Street – two-storeys with dormer in attic

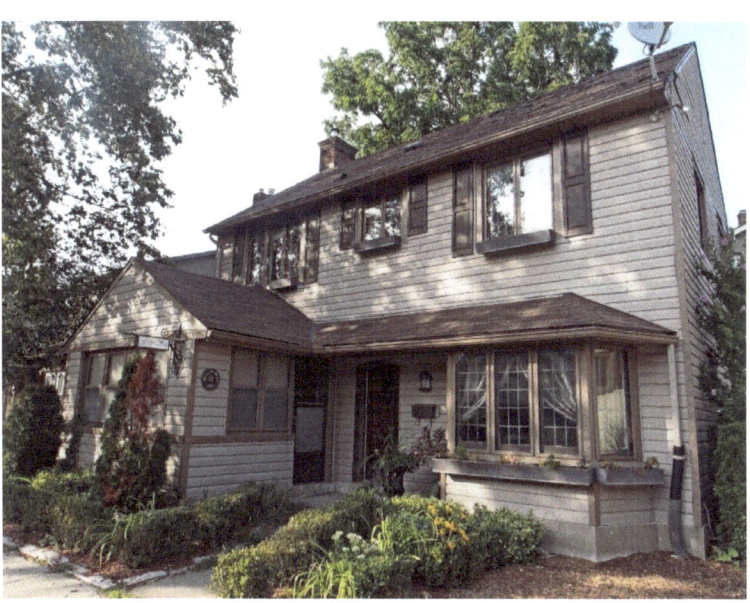

56 Yates Street

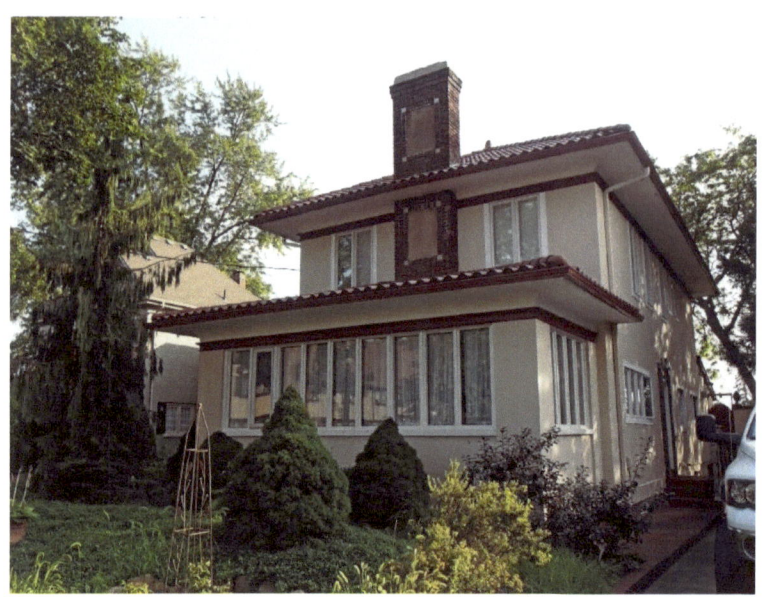

Yates Street

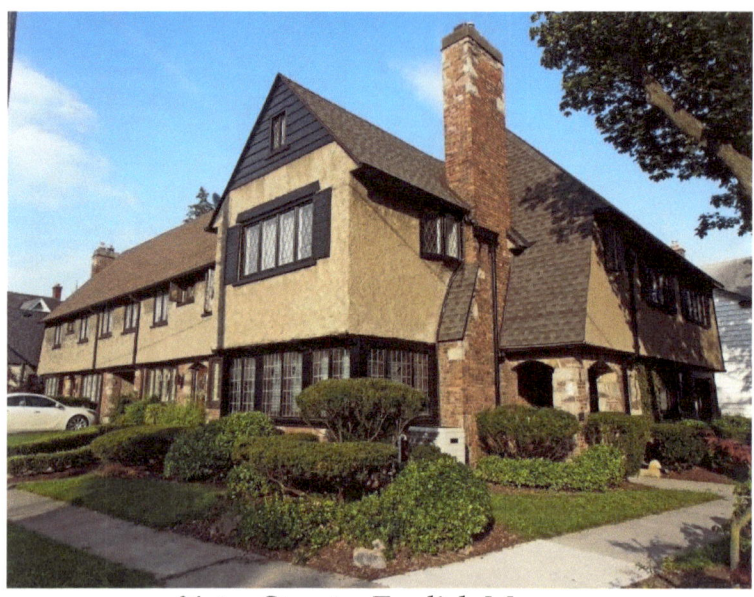

Yates Street – English Manor

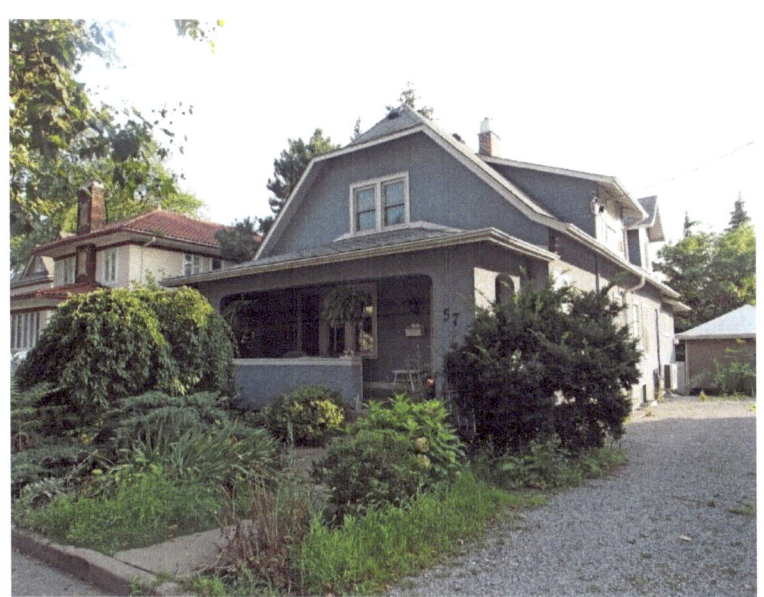

57 Yates Street – chipped gable, dormers

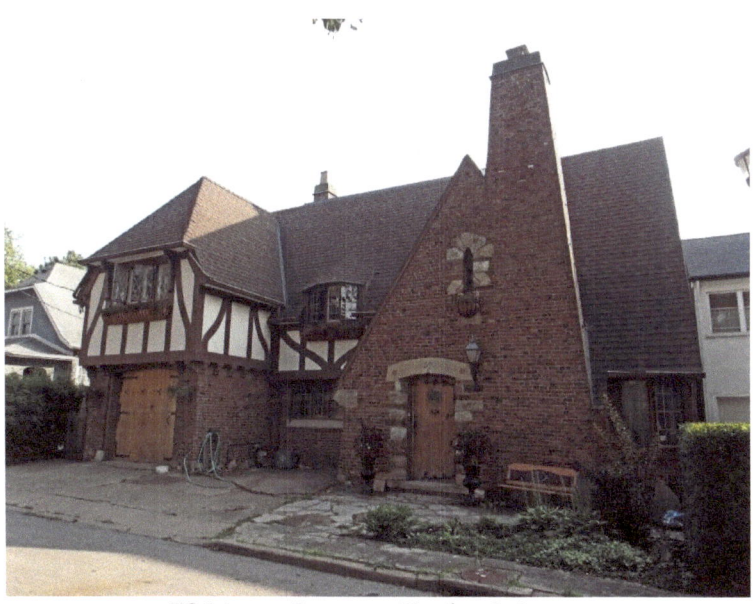

59 Yates Street – Tudor Manor

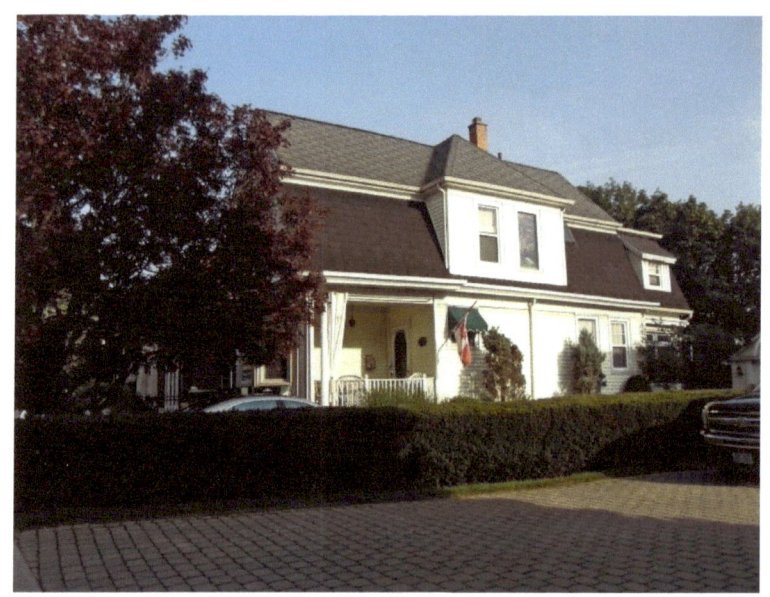

Yates Street

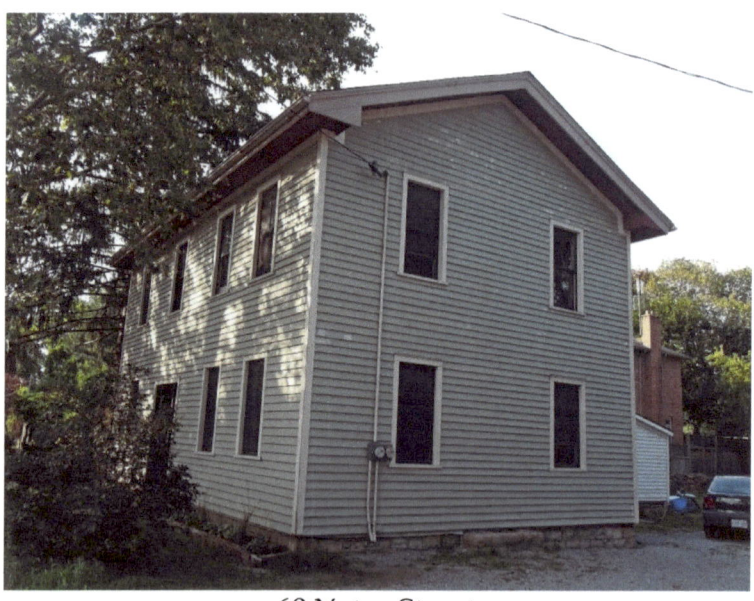

60 Yates Street

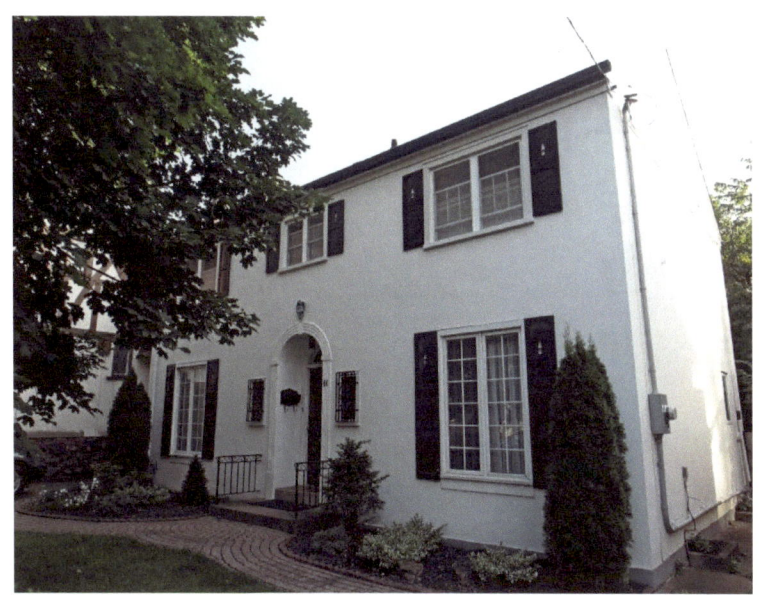

61 Yates Street – gable roof

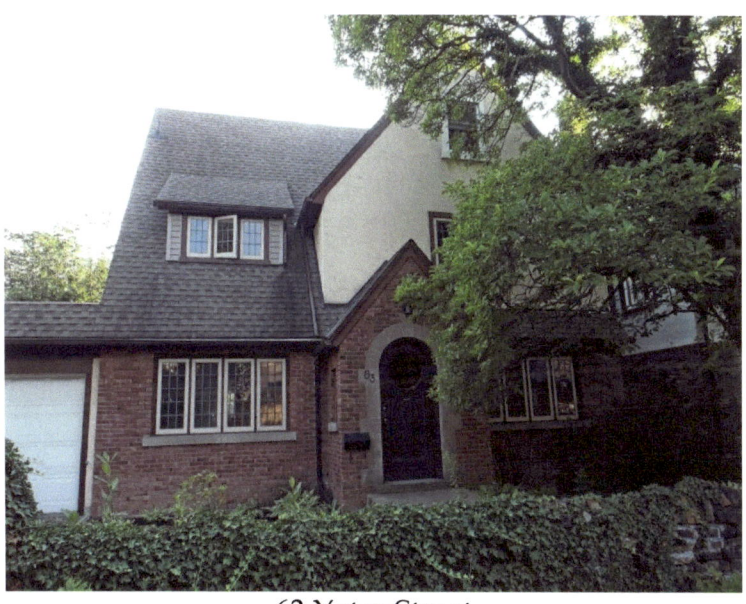

63 Yates Street

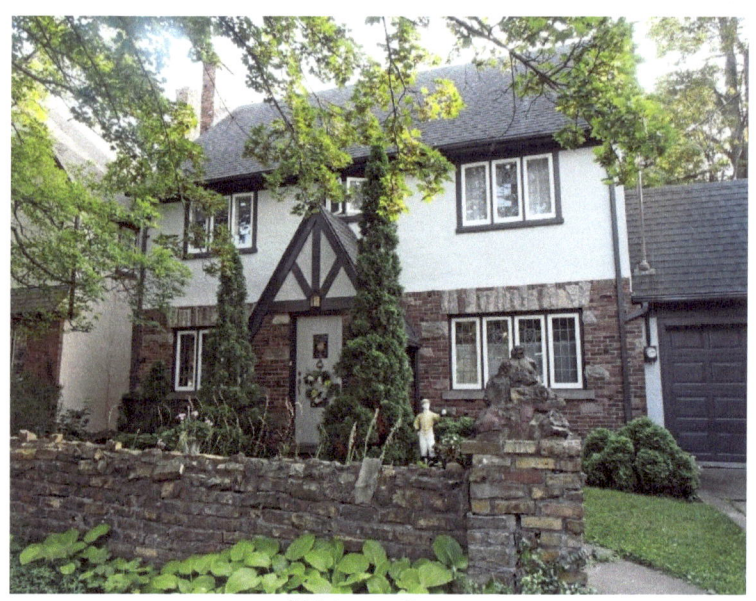
65 Yates Street

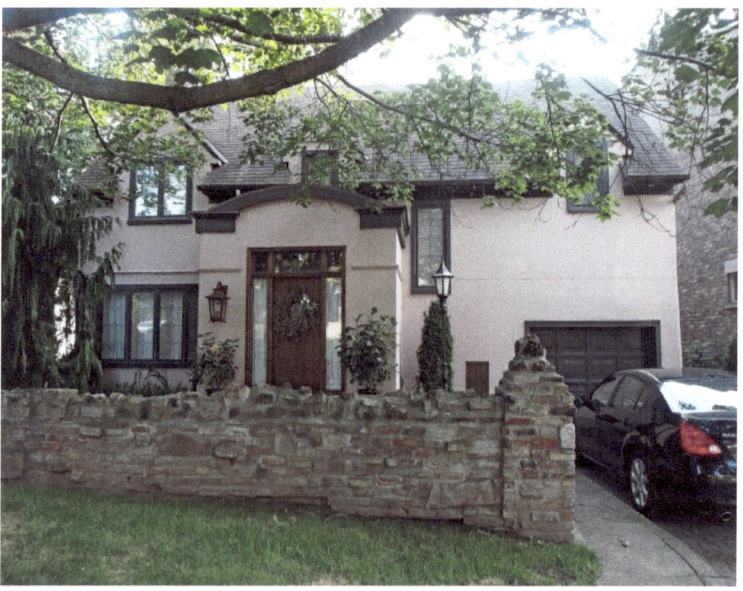
Yates Street

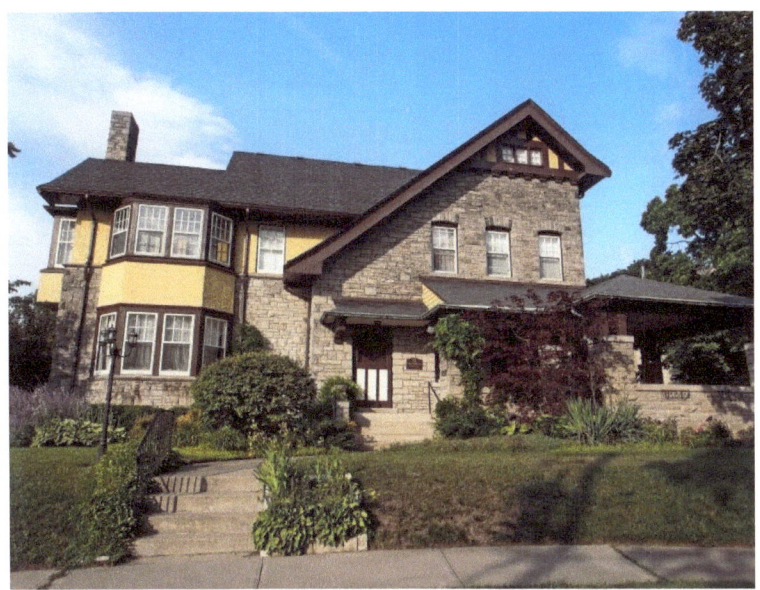

68 Yates Street – Springbank House – Vernacular

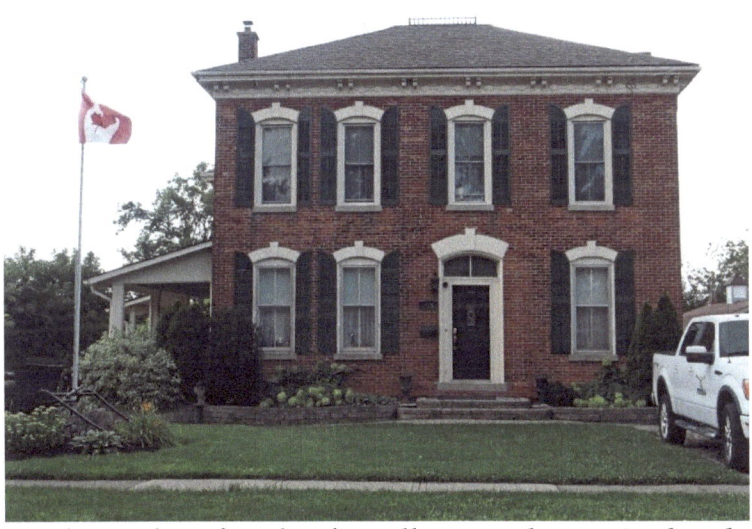

#115 – hipped roof widow's walk on peak, cornice brackets, keystones, shutters, transom window

Architectural Terms

Bay Window: A window that projects out from a wall, in a semicircular, rectangular, or polygonal design. Used frequently in Gothic and Victorian designs. Example: 59 Queen Street, Page 14	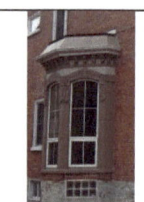
Brackets: a decorative or weight-bearing structural element which forms a right angle with one side against a wall and the other under a projecting surface such as an eave or roof. Example: 11 Welland Avenue, Page 36	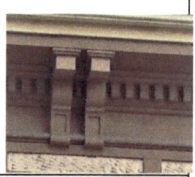
Buttress: a masonry structure built against or projecting from a wall which serves to support or reinforce the wall. In Canadian architecture, they are sometimes used for decoration. Example: 31 Chestnut Street East, Page 12	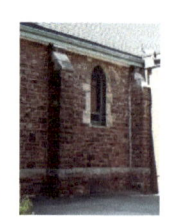
Capital: The uppermost finish or decoration on a column. A Doric column is characterized by a plain column with no base, a shaft with twenty flutings, and a simple capital with a simple entablature. Example: 101 St. Paul Street, Page 22 A Composite is a mixture of two or sometimes, three, of the major styles Doric, Ionic, and Corinthian. Example: 26 Yates Street, Page 45	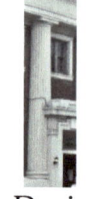 Doric 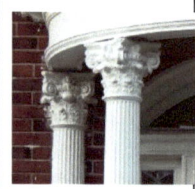 Composite

Corbel: Corbelling is the original method of making arches a series of stones or bricks that protrude beyond the lower level to finally cover the arch. Corbels are used to support cornices, turrets, brackets, ribs and oriel windows. A corbel is also a stone or piece of wood that supports a super incumbent weight. Example: 57 Queen Street, Page 13	
Cupola: A domed or curved roof rising from a building as a decorative element. Example: Yates Street, Page 40	
Dentil Moulding: an even series of rectangles used as ornamental decoration in cornices. Example: Court Street, Page 10	
Dormer: (French for "sleep") a gable end window that pierces through the plane of a sloping roof surface to create usable space in the top floor or attic of a building by adding headroom. Example: 27 Yates Street, Page 45	
Entrance: The entrance encompasses the doorway and the inner vestibule or, in residential architecture, the covered porch. Example: 26 Yates Street, Page 45	

Gable: the triangular portion of a wall between the edges of a sloping roof. Example: 21 Thomas Street, Page 35	
Gambrel Roof: a symmetrical two-sided roof with two slopes on each side; the upper slope is positioned at a shallow angle, while the lower slope is steep. It is similar to a mansard roof, but a gambrel has vertical gable ends instead of being hipped at the four corners of the building. Example: 10 Thomas Street, Page 34	
Hipped Roof: a roof where all sides slope downwards to the walls with no gables. Example: 35 Yates Street, Page 50	
Keystones and Voussoirs: a voussoir is a wedge-shaped element used in building an arch. A keystone is the central stone that locks all the stones into position, allowing the arch to bear weight. A keystone is often enlarged and embellished. Example: 38 Yates Street, Page 51	
Lancet Window: a tall, narrow window with a pointed arch at its top. Example: 31 Chestnut Street East, Page 12	

Mansard Roof: This style was popularized by Francois Mansart (1598-1666), an accomplished architect of the French Baroque period and especially fashionable during the Second French Empire (1852-1870). This roof is almost flat on the top section, with two slopes on each of its sides with the lower slope at a steeper angle than the upper, and has dormer windows. Example: 15 Welland Avenue, Page 36	
Palladian Window: a large window that is divided into three sections with the centre section larger than the two side sections and usually arched. Example: 9 Welland Avenue, Page 35	
Parapet: low wall around the edge of a roof. Example: St. Paul Street, Page 29	
Pediment: a triangular section above the door or portico, usually supported by columns. The inside of the triangle is called the tympanum. Example: 18 Yates Street, Page 40	
Quoin: masonry blocks at the corner of a wall, often a decorative feature, usually larger or of a different colour than the rest of the wall. Example: St. Paul Street, Page 18	
Sidelight: a vertical window that flanks a door, and is often used to emphasize the importance of a primary entrance. **Transom Window:** the light above the doorway, also called a fanlight. Example: 31 Yates Street, Page 48	

Tower: A circular, square, or octagonal vertical structure higher than the surrounding structure that is usually part of an existing building and is created either for extra defense or for a specific purpose such as a clock or a bell tower. Example: 321 St. Paul Street, Page 31	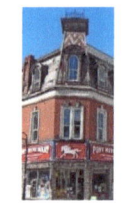
Turret: a small tower that projects from the wall of a building. Example: 22 Academy Street, Page 6	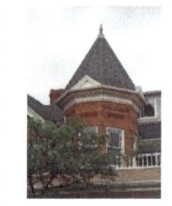
Verge board and Finial: also called bargeboards – hang from the projecting end of a roof and are often elaborately carved and ornamented. **Finial:** ornament added to the top of a gable, pinnacle, canopy or spire – a Gothic element. Example: 152 Welland Avenue, Page 37	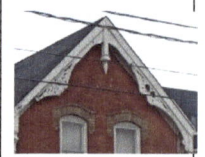
Window Hood: A **hood** is the piece found above window openings, usually of an ornate design, and covers the top third of the opening. Hoods are commonly placed above arched or curved openings on both windows and doors. Example: 12 Yates Street, Page 41	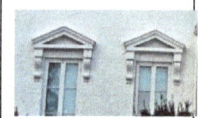

Building Styles

Classical Revival, 1820-1860 – This style was an analytical, scientific, and dogmatic revival based on intensive studies of Greek and Roman buildings, concerned with the application of Greek plans and proportions to civic buildings. Schools, libraries, government offices, and most other civic buildings were built in the Classical Revival style. The white columned porches of the Classical Revival domestic buildings are identified with the mansions of wealthy land owners in Canada. Example: 26 Yates Street, Page 45	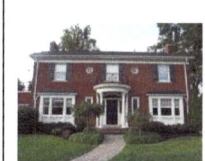
Edwardian, 1900-1930 – This style bridges the ornate and elaborate styles of the Victorian era and the simplified styles of the 20th century. Edwardian Classicism provided simple, balanced facades, simple rooflines, dormer windows, large front porches, and smooth brick surfaces. Voussoirs and keystones are used sparingly and are understated. Finials and cresting are absent. Cornice brackets and braces are block-like and openings have flat arches or plain stone lintels. Example: 28 Yates Street, Page 46	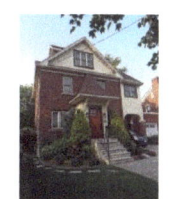
Georgian, before 1860 – This style began with the British King Georges in the 18th century. These buildings have balanced facades around a central door, medium-pitched gable roofs, and small paned windows. Example: 29 Yates Street, Page 47	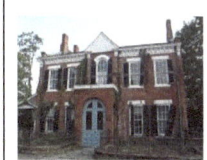

Gothic Revival, 1830-1890 – These decorative buildings have sharply-pitched gables with highly detailed verge boards, pointed-arch window openings, and dichromatic brickwork. It is a common style in Ontario. Example: 87 Queen Street, Page 16	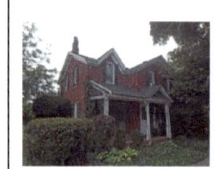
An English country house is a large house or mansion usually unfortified. Example: Yates Street, Page 58	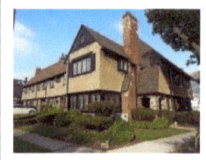
Neo-colonial (also Colonial Revival, Georgian Revival or Neo-Georgian) architecture seeks to revive elements of architectural style of American colonial architecture of the period around the Revolutionary War which drew strongly from Georgian architecture of Great Britain. Architecture from the 18th and early 19th centuries in Ontario includes a wide assortment of detailing and ornament applied to a design centered around the fireplace and the source of water. Structures are typically two stories, have a symmetrical front facade with elaborate front doorways, often with decorative crown pediments, fanlights, and sidelights, symmetrical windows flanking the front entrance, often in pairs or threes, and columned porches. Example: 10 Thomas Street, Page 34	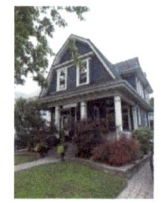

Regency Cottage, 1830-1860 – This style originated in England in 1815 and spread to Ontario later in the 19th century as British officers retired to Canada. It is a modest one-storey house with a low-pitched hip roof and has a symmetrical front façade. Example: 31 Yates Street, Page 48	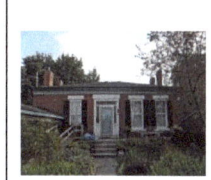
Second Empire, 1860-1880 – The mansard roof is the most noteworthy feature of this style and is evidence of the French origins. Projecting central towers and one or two-storey bays can also be present. Example: 15 Welland Avenue, Page 36	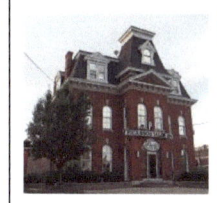
Tudor Revival – exposed timbers with stucco infill, multi-paned windows. Example: 23 Yates Street, Page 44	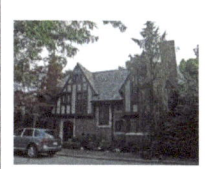
Vernacular/Traditional Mode 1638 - 1950 Influenced but not defined by a particular style, vernacular buildings are made from easily available materials and exhibit local design characteristics. Example: 68 Yates Street, Page 63	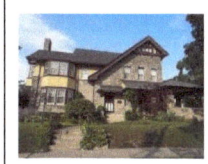

www.ingramcontent.com/pod-product-compliance
Lightning Source LLC
Chambersburg PA
CBHW040230220526

45473CB00001B/193